North Dakota is Everywhere

AN ANTHOLOGY OF CONTEMPORARY
NORTH DAKOTA POETS

North Dakota is Everywhere

AN ANTHOLOGY OF CONTEMPORARY
NORTH DAKOTA POETS

Edited by Heidi Czerwiec

Published by the Institute for Regional Studies Press
North Dakota State University
Dept. 2360, P.O. Box 6050, Fargo, ND 58108-6050.
www.ndsu.edu/ahss/ndirs

North Dakota is Everywhere:
An Anthology of Contemporary North Dakota Poets
Edited by Heidi Czerwiec

Cover image and author photo courtesy Britta Trygstad.
Book design by Deb Tanner.

International Standard Book Number: 978-0-911042-81-8
Library of Congress Control Number: 2015935251
Printed in the United States.

To Wyatt,
my own best poem and
piece of North Dakota.

Contents

Introduction

The source of poetry—of verse—is agricultural, from the Old English *fers*, from Latin *versus,* "a turn of the plow, a furrow, a line of writing." That North Dakota and poetry should be brought together in this anthology is perhaps both improbable and fate. Improbable because such turning in North Dakota has always been a struggle. Plowing the sod of the Plains was back-breaking. People live in distant towns, sometimes completely cut off from each other by winter blizzards or by summer responsibilities. Literary communities become difficult to maintain.

But poets persevere and, once planted in the rich soil, thrive—which is why it's not surprising that in Old English, *fers* also means "to befall; fate." Like many others, the story of how I arrived in North Dakota is full of a number of such fated turnings. In making my home here, I have come to love my adopted state and its community of writers. So I was surprised to discover that, while several of this state's poets have been included in various regional Midwestern anthologies, no unique collection exists that celebrates the work of North Dakota poets. This book hopes to remedy that lack.

To compile this anthology, I settled on the following criteria: contemporary North Dakota poets would be defined as those who 1) are alive and writing, 2) have published a volume of poetry of at least 25 pages and 3) were born in and/or have lived in North Dakota for at least 10 years. With this standard in mind, I started contacting writers. I immediately was humbled by the enthusiastic and grateful responses I received. The poets agreed that such an anthology was long overdue, were thankful for my interest and were excited to participate.

What struck me about the poems that I received, and about the poets themselves, was the range represented. The poets in this collection write in free verse lines by turns both terse and expansive, in the finely wrought formal verse of sestinas and sonnets, and in the tense patter of spoken word. Some of these poems first appeared in print nearly half a century ago; some appear first within these pages.

Sure, there were poems on the expected subjects: the North Dakota landscape, family heritage and the weather, in particular the brutal winters. But the work in this anthology demonstrates remarkable scope and nuance.

There are poets descended from the High Plains' indigenous inhabitants, and from those who emigrated here—whether from Germany, Russia or the Scandinavian countries in the 19th century, or more recently from other parts of the country and world.

They write about the historical struggles of settlement and assimilation, and about more contemporary versions of those struggles in the Bakken oil patch in the western part of the state. Some write about North Dakota from the rural settings they have known and loved for a lifetime, others from the distant vantages of nostalgia or escape, and still others from the point of view of transplants coming to terms with their new home, as I did.

The poets here include seasoned and emerging voices, women and men, old and young, those from the ranching and oil-flared Badlands west of the Missouri, and from the flood-prone river valley farmlands of the east.

To return to the origins of poetry, when the epic poet Homer has the hero Odysseus declare that "day after day I ache to reach home," he coins the term "nostalgia," from the Greek *algia* "ache" and *nostos* "homecoming." The poems in this book ache for home. They ache to be at home. In writing about those who ache in this great expanse, these poets write about what connects us together as humans, poems that sing to each other across lines and pages and space, demonstrating that, as poet Thomas McGrath asserts in his *Letter to an Imaginary Friend*, North Dakota is everywhere.

Many thanks and high-fives go to Aaron Poochigian for goading me to pursue what was originally an offhand comment about the lack of a North Dakota anthology, to Brenna Daugherty Gerhardt of the North Dakota Humanities Council for praising my obsessiveness and calling it "ambition," to Ross Collins and the board of the North Dakota Institute for Regional Studies Press for accepting this project and seeing it through to publication, and to the many presses who generously granted me permission to reprint work. To my husband, Evan, for supporting every damn fool idea I have, and to my son Wyatt, my own little piece of North Dakota. And, of course, I want to thank all of the poets who contributed their beautiful poems to this collection. I hope you enjoy the experience of this book as much as I did.

Heidi Czerwiec
Associate Professor of English
University of North Dakota

Richard Watson

The River of the Milky Way

—after Tom McGrath, in these Oil Wars

1. *Live on to the Milky Way*

Ah the air of Terra, Venus and Mars,
under the sweep of giant wings,
unseen, but vortex powered all the same:
chimes all clang,
3 note 2 step tunes in warp drive swing—
I lean to the Northwest in an (only a northern song, George)
immeasurable wind—
Passionate fools,
rubbed raw with repeated imagined
selves, none of whom are us!
All the stink is blown away—

I find myself the color of mud—
Love, for us, is never enough,
and still it is all you will have—

The long shadows ride beneath
the invisible wings above you,
across the hill tops and away—
The valley below is dark,
lighted windows in houses taunt us all—
Walk down, stand still, no matter—
There is streak of gold
right across the lines of your face—
Die? We all must, weak in that light,
and live on to the Milky Way

* * *

He's a clean old man, headed down to Pickle-dilly circus—

He has some songs he wants to play down there—

Bison steaks and pickled ice fished pickerel

Cannot save a soul—

But he eats them whole and yearns for

Bronze Age tales to take him home—they will—

Grandma's down by the open garden gate

2. *Mandolins of the West River*

I wrote the supernatural love story set in Noorrrtth Daakohtah—
Named it "The Ballads from The Spot"
you are in the Oil Wars now—and you, old mandolin,
and your odd Bronze-Aged holy woman, and your kool aid
popcorn Twilight dead Zone jokes,
But I think it had another name—I think we all have had another name—
Now is the time to make
the book a movie of this love, oily proportion, golden light,

Redemption stuck in the color of mud,
from a man's own veins and blood, bleeding out into the earth of
the west—the pumps on
pads release the natural gas, and the black little fossil cells,

the geologic souls, ten billion
plants and animals wait these resurrections and sweet remembrances!
And less wretched new conditions—

In the mean, these times are mean,

time, we will be on bench out on the porch, and the mandolin,
guitar and harp will chime like older
broken church bells made of wood and wire, out across the valley and plains
into the bowels of God's creation schemes;

we drink red wine in the wind, the sun, last summer's late,

Imagined feast, milk and honey-bread-song tunes,

Milk and honey bread beneath the highways made of stars

* * *

Was a fool young man, never did get to Woodstock—

Now he sings and guards the open garden gate—

"Water, that's where I came from now," he sings

"I can feel it when I wash my face,

When I float out on the muddy lake,

When I shower Sam Scratchy stinky nights away."

His songs are air, born near the ancient lilac bush—

Grandma helps him guard that garden gate

3. *St. Bridget Saves St. Valentine*

May the bloody little arrows of fat-assed little cupids
prick your dickery sense, affectations too, cocked tocks of time
in praise of that rebel Roman Sarge, "oh yester and oh yore,"

Who refused to fight the wars no more, no more, no sword and shield—
whom they tied to a post and shot full of bolts until
he bled like the broken-hearted love he was—
Their sinful darts, not a stinking one that missed the mark,
and they shall repent in the Eros' arms: eternity,
while the Great "I Am" makes them listen on: "More Harps!"
While all us crooked archers, repentant, rose-pricked
wrong-shot sinners, belly up to the chocolate bar,
bubbly wine, where the fountains flow with
holy Bridget's homemade honey beer,
and she was no mean sharp archer then, herself—Blessed Days!
And the minstrels sing us all the green sweet songs

* * *

"There's another tale," says he who plays on Main Street,

High Plains Creole at the Bookstore doors,

And if it's late and weather waits,

You'll see he guards the open garden gate

Beneath the blue stars spread across the hills and sky—

Grandma sleeps in the rocking chair beneath the blue star sky

4. *Gumbo to the Kingdom*

The church is a twin to ancient Norse-built walls,
but could be seen as a temple too, Mount Fuji's sacred side,
or some temple up on Red Pine's old Cold Mountain—
At the top of seven ascending roofs we see a spire,
a spar-like lance, the shaft of a great harpoon,
four fire dragon head reliefs,
8 carved wooden crosses that St Patrick might have known—
small winged dragons carved in wood beneath the seven leveled roofs—

a waning half-moon floats, 10 on Sunday Morning—
Within a few years, China will sport some millions of re-born Christians—
It's fire works again—

We profane the Sabbath, so the Prophet says,
when we do not care of the hungry, poor, oppressed—
when poets tell no stories, high school English teachers
assign work sheets: allegory, symbol, or metaphor—

When I was 7, Percy and I almost dug a hole to China
but we had to go home for supper—Jesus was down there—
the late Summer sun went down, and the devil came and filled our hole—
Percy and I will dig through gumbo—We will turn the color of oil—

What are the songs he plays to guard the garden gate?

* * *

5.

In and out of the color crashed clear definition tipsy talking heads,

election night wizards craft hysteria as an art—
the chemicals ooze; nerve endings zing
in the blood of the body political—peace—the bacteria,
introduced into the republic's spacious heart space
by an unknown carrier host; yes that bug,
too small for naked light (just the slight fever now)—
this bacteria looms the size of the horror of Hades
on the slide beneath the scope in the
hospital lab—bacteria, fuzz, fur like the tall
pasture stink weed, yellow and wet and clotted
with snow in the "seasonal mix," the bit of ice
that yanks the car towards the ditch: pull back!

Heal this land, the mind, the memory, the broken promise,
the miracle changes to hubris so fast—
God does move in mysterious ways; let's
not dare to make decisions for her at all

* * *

The minstrels of the Milky Way sing on—

And once out there the song ain't gone—

The Gumbo Poet, Golem-like, that heavy WORD

Gets up and walks the Garden paths:

North Dakota, somewhere near the Milky Way

6. *Is That Our Mother's Voice?*

BOOM, and gold shoots in through the cath,
like a mutant chemo-brained junkie's dream,
wake up and radiate one more day—
"Harvest and planting" as if you were back on the plow
down on the South Dakota line,
but now it's the temple of healing in a Minnesota valley that slowly
empties its October paint can colors
into the river and brings on
the thunder, lighting and cold rain, so the lightning flashes against
the black mirror windows
of the Temple Complex sky line, and the dark windows reflect
the light that still will grow
even stronger on mornings after
the winter slips in on the clipper ship of white cloud and wind
from the Canadian ocean and across the Dakota sea—
Show us all a song to sing—a pizza and a bottle of red
can heal like Jesus' hands—Is that our Mother's voice we hear?

Is she turned the color of mud?

"...and the Word became flesh
and pitched a tent in our midst,
full of grace and truth,"

Somewhere below the sky highways

And the Gumbo Poet sleeps all day

While the death dealing songs still guard the garden gate

7.

The Gumbo Golem is made of sod and blue stem, wild rose bush,
sandstone, prickly pear, so flesh is the color of magical mud—
The Gumbo Golem will come, stride across the crude oil slicks,
the sloppy spills, the carcass, small farms, homesteads
into the Oil Wars, to crunch and grind the metal, pumps,
the pads, the fractured limestone bones of earth,
and there will be an end to the obscene times—go to your bar
or church of your choice, go to the digital blue screen trance;
vote for the bearded asses who poison your earth with your money,
the dimple-chinned boar hound you think will protect your homes,
but the Golem is coming, and the ocean, the inland sea,
the glacial ghosts of clean, high-aired blue-iced heaven,
they rise up from the past and scrub and wash this bit of
the garden clean and start the process of redemption up again

Grandma, where has the young man gone,

The one who sang those Beatle songs at the garden gates?

8. *Just Like That*

"I tend not to trust my intuitions about the presence of spiritual beings,
even when a force like a microwave signal fires through me, or when I
sense my mother or father."
    —Larry Woiwode, *What I Think I Did*

I sit on the love seat and look

At the sun go, only 5:42

On a January day—

The light is in my eyes—

I get up, walk to the kitchen

And then walk back—

The sun is gone behind the hill,

Like that

The trainer plane from the

Airstrip, a single prop,

Comes grinding across

My favorite sky: sound again

(Next the chorus of honking geese)—

The plane flies west to east

Across a clear and dark blue wall

Of sky in stillness I can

Never seem to comprehend

In this noisy, gassed up, combusted town—

The winged black silhouette

Looks as though it's headed

Straight at the half-full moon,

Southwest as the river valley runs—

At the last second it just

Guns it motor and slides

Right past the knife edge of the moon—

"Just like that," I hear my mother say—

Her voice is years away

And speaks right in my ear

All the way to here

From where she's seated next to God—

Just like that, I know that she is there,

Is here, but where in where am I,

And more a mystery,

Where in whom or who are you?

The engine drones away;

Eggbeater engine fades to black—

Just like that I say again

Just like that, I hear

My mother—did you never meet?

She laughs out loud at us right now—

Finally if you looked,

A star—the few clouds against the west

Don't stretch like Homer's fingers

But streak and tear instead,

Not shook foil like Hopkins,

But soft cream-cotton cloth:

First yellow, yellow-gold-to pink,

Then rose, and finally, plumes of plume

To deeper purple, maroon,

Dark as dense and shadowed leaves

Into blue-black, and then

Simply clouds again,

Here with me, the last of light

Just as almost dark,

As dark as the hill beneath the sky,

And now black behind

The darkest edge between the earth, air,

Sky and cloud of the lined-out curve of hill,

Then lighter, for a moment, clearer still,

And finally if you look, a star

Oh, again, that one Blue Star

No telescope can name it then or now—

9. 50 Years Ago Today: Sing the Devil Down

Cod's own trute—what the 'ell 'ave Maria I missed?
I was sitting making a WW2 Spitfire model
mellow on chips and eggs and glue—
mum and dad out somewhere on the moors
playing at long hands of cutthroat whist
when the Beatles come on that gangster Sullivan,
and by God they high jacked my back beat
and saved my soul for something other than Vietnam—
and now here I am, 50 years gone,
hair still too long, Rubber Soul crazed
Revolver the only weapon I trust,
and when does the Magical Mystery change?
I can't seem to let it be
but where is the place that we can go?
I can see the road from the empty chair—
I imagine all kinds of lovely songs

and learn them all and write them down
and digitally resurrect their birth,
but where oh where do we go, Lads and Ladies—
Good night, the banker said to me—
Good night, said the queen of spades—
the fisher king is in a net—
it's iron cold and almost Lent—
the world is here and so we must go sing!

It's off we go to the Oil Wars,

And here will come them songs we sing my Dears!

North Dakota is...

10. *The River of the Milky Way*

A man and woman I know well

Are plotting out the hillside down the

Road from me for homes,

A home they haven't built,

The home they lost a year or so ago

in the greatest flood we've seen—

We don't need an allegory to grasp this tale—

This tale is allegory on the lizard's bone—

A doe and fawn I met today

Looked in through the window from my lawn

And then just ambled on across the

Yard and up the coulee in the trees

After the flood that was the meanest flood we've seen—

Dragonflies and Monarchs loop against

The tail wind of the only Northwest breeze we've had

As displaced creatures of the valley

Slowly climb up hill to us,

And my Grandma tries to keep her flowers

All alive with water from the flood,

Flowers that she moved here to the higher ground

All this is the allegory or the proverb we call mystery:

"The One Who Is" is not the one we thought;

I AM! Is not the thing we think,

Not the she-he-it we may have made—

Look beyond and see the glimmer and the gleam—

Glimpse the King and Queen of Heaven's wild domain—

The lesson is the river that will always rise again,

And the river of the Milky Way that we will always sail—

North Dakota is not a Greek Island

It is a small sweet peninsula of the Milky Way

* * *

11. *He Picks a Black Guitar*

In between the red rocks

Beneath a sliced half moon

(Yes, moon again, and night)

We say here's the crime, committed now in

This empty godless city,

Bound in blood and red rock walls,

Spaced, carved from blood stone meat

We see the half moon fall

To nowhere—we are here again-

Where is the detective in our need?

There is still no need to hide—

Old man Song has seen it all—

He picks a black guitar

And sings a song: "North Dakota is..."

Benediction

I wanna sit in the sun at Grandma's garden gate,

sit and play guitar,

have a woman and child walk by not even know who they are

share my song with their bread and cheese

my bottle of red wine

hear that woman sing the ancient tongue

see the fire in the child's eyes

the fire of holy Wisdom's ancient new born eye,

and feel the fire in between my notes

...everywhere is here

Larry Woiwode

Crystals

O my brother, remember North Dakota,
The nights of angular snow, the drift of
Snow that rose until it reached our window-
Sill, and then rose slowly up the glass; below
Its fuming surface, visible through the glass,
The quiet crystals—glittering, blue, serene.
Remember the ribbed trough of ice that guided
Our rocketing sled down past roots, stumps, stones,
A culvert—you on the bottom, me on the top, knocking
Your breath out—down the steep bank to the uneven flat-
Lands of the frozen lake below, skimming across its ripples,
The sled slapping down hard like the hull of a light boat, taking
Us far out onto the lake, farther out than we should have gone,
Then slowly slowing to a stop. In its white center,
                    Silence.

                    Spring,
The dry and transparent air. The buffalo grass we pulled up from
Around the rabbit pen, the way it squeaked in our hands, a green
Sound. Remember Mary Liffert, the widowed neighbor who
Made us kneel beside her rocker and pray *The Hail Mary*,
The dignified rock she adopted while we did, the lodge
We made by tunneling under the pile of brush, our talks
Beneath its network of limbs, then silence, your back-
Lit eyes absorbed in a conversation beyond me, quiet,
Serene. *You*. O my brother, remember North Dakota,
The glacial boulders piled up in the shape of a boat,
Visible above the waves of wheat, sailing—*Where?*
Out of North Dakota, out of that country, out of
Childhood to now. But O my brother, above all,
Remember these small beginnings, these
Crystals, or I might have invented our love.

DEAR
NEW,

daughter
number one,
an intuition can be
the hardest part of per-
ception to receive, laced as it is
with latent prophecy, if prophecy
is the proper term, or love, either's
meaning as loose as November rain,
so when I walk the coils and conduits
of a mat that once was swaying stems
and leavings of liquid green in late July
and now is straw, dead and hempen dry,
I sense a further field, not of stratagems,
as a tooth-nerve-jolt from ten years back
fires its ghost-ganglia-hits down memory
to the original jaw-widening throes below
a present tinfoil voltage—in this way I see
in a noisy rush a stand of rye in Michigan
collapse into a mass of conduits like these
before it doubled itself in yield and growth
that very spring (for rye must die to yield),
as now with steady steps on straw I know
that this grain, too, will root and resurrect,
sway with liquid green, and at that I know
that you will rise beyond your present want
of self-defense toward heaven's blue decree
like grain, and any hurt or work of the world
that tended not cheer you on—or so I thought
you thought, way back when—finally will unfurl
and set you springing free as an athlete who exerts
a league of greater will to leap the everyday, a boxer of the
quality of Ali, in early training, skipping rope—a similar noisy ease.
That is my word on this and how I picture your ringing green release,

   DEAR
YOU.

Horses

Horses sleep in the wind driven snow northwest
out of Fargo. Flocks of buntings come down in
swirls of flakes into fields of stalks. Night
appears an hour ahead this early March. Thick
flakes darken and slow. Slush forms on the horses'
backs. They shudder it free, steam, are cold once
more, stamp, let it build up. No colors now show.
Great heads droop toward drifts climbing up dark
hocks as silence ferries in its crystalline blow:

Out of Fargo, apart from you across a curve of
continent this season, seeing snow fall over
these of all the sleeping horses here between.

Son Night

And then you'll pick this up,
As it devolves through time,
And see I thought of you
That late fall day, my room
A distance from the one
You occupied at night
As though to hold yourself
Attentive to the time
Or hold yourself in place,
Perhaps, a nightly hope
That words will be a help
To you to work a set
That are your own and might
Be welcoming to me
When I return—the wind
A rooftree overhead,
A ridge whose semblance is
A structure like my voice,
Its tones amenable
To you, I hope. If so, I,
The ridge in metaphor,
Propel my words across
This page to let you know
I thought of you and how
The coming years will place
A child in your arms, your
Son; and when you hear
The semblance of a wind,
A ridge or rooftree speak,
You'll hear the word I meant,
Son, son, son, son, son...

And then you'll pick this up.

December 10
Sixty-Two

The exalted language that you say I use
To depict a slight in universal hues
Has left me breath enough, I think, to say—

No, I can't. I can't employ a display
Of words like balloons in rattling flatulence
Going flat, create the showy elements
That pristine nature surely serves you up—
So I suck all that back in and both lungs cup
Up air, alveoli bulging brimful, my sides
Expanding wide as blue balloons—which divides
The frothing pace engendered two by two, so
In primal sexual lather I let it blow,
Stem squealing, rounded cheeks going gray-blue
And wheeze out two overused words: *Love! You!*

Madelyne Camrud

The Day after Valentine's

In late-afternoon traffic, a balloon,
like a heart blown in from somewhere,
crosses the street in front of our car.
I want to stop, run after it, at least turn
for a last look as it passes behind us.
But I am the driver now, you, my passenger,
we travel one way. I follow our lane
at a safe speed, stopping only for a red light.

The heart floats further into the distance,
the string a hand once held, trailing,
still attached. I try hard not to look back.
There's little we can say or do,
cannot retrieve what is lost.

The errant heart drifts aimlessly.

How It Begins

Winter is endless when you're in it, long cold stays,
blue snow stretches every direction.

You head out for groceries in a thick coat
and find the store is not there.

You spend the night making hot tea you never drink.
Carelessness got you here, you didn't prepare.

You've forgotten, in spite of everything,
you were too caught up in living.

It happened slowly like a marriage unwinding comfortably,
staying inside, turning on fires with a remote.

Try as you might you can't get back that last summer,
nothing can change the Arctic water

that separates you like an animal on an ice floe.
Now the long nights grow longer. You like them for their sleep,

the dreams with slippery hands, one with a man who tossed
a little girl repeatedly into the air,

caught her before that last time when he missed.

A White Ring around the Moon

The radio warning fifty degrees below zero,
we're tuned to news: bats in Vermont found frozen
in the snow, noses ringed white, a symptom
of whatever it was that wiped them out.
They forgot the way to their caves like bees
in Texas forgot their hives. A keeper told me
last summer they wandered aimlessly over clover
like lost jet pilots, as if something in the universe
had changed their radar. And you, love,
                                    loose in clover

or out in the cold, would not find your way home—
I know this. Once you ran out, didn't come back
when I called, brushed me off like a mosquito
when I caught up. But, tonight, unlike bees and bats,
we cohabit in ways they cannot. Warmed by a heart vent,
not working as hard for good, we are just hanging around,
                                    under the moon,
its ring a sign the cold will stay a long time.

Watching

We know all about time now,
how it speeds, how it slows,

the way that one season closes,
then opens to another, the days

a ball of twine growing larger
on the prairie. We know

about moments like this, when
my husband and I put bird seed

in the feeder, then sit, side
by side, at a table to watch,

feeling as serene as we have
in any church. We bear

resemblance, in this small act
to acceptance, perhaps forgiving

what we know of each other,
of growing older. The birds

know our shadows well, yet
they flutter, diving in and out

so quickly from the window,
not yet trusting as we trust

the mercies of bread crumbs and seeds.

The Bird in My House

A small bird slept in my house last night.
Some may doubt it but I swear
I found him like an oversized moth
fluttering against the glass, kitchen window.
Couldn't shoo him out
though I tried again and again.
The bird, smarter than I, more nimble,
stopped high atop a cupboard I could not reach—
nothing to do but let him roost.

                The season late,
wind and rain had changed the trees.
If I were a bird, I'd have sought shelter, too.
As it was, I went out for the evening,
and, home again, found the bird nowhere,
a truth that refused to come to light.
Upstairs in bed, I imagined him,
head tucked under a wing, sleeping
the way you rested, head on your arm,
beside me. I turned over and tried to sleep,
but all I could think of was the bird.

                I wondered again
how he found his way into my house,
come not at all like a thief, more like

whatever it is that breathes love into the night.

Dale Jacobson

A Moment of Clarity

The leaves were green flame.

The birch tree was a white journey
from dark water to clear sky,
roots to radiance.

The crow was a long echo that took flight.

I Keep Returning

(excerpt from *A Walk by the River*)

I keep returning to earlier times, called
by my home town where I once walked
in light so familiar I felt invisible and whole
—and followed the river gleaming and cool,
its dark waters rippling its mysterious word
through the ways and turns of my seasons.

What have I lost that I keep hunting my past,
called by some earlier dawn, mystified by moon?

And once walking a path like this one
came upon fallen wings, dusty, a hawk
evicted from the shifting rooms of sky.
And thought then how all worries
in time are equalized by the wind,
in time the light hunts all hawks down
darkly in the gloaming where the widening
wings of all shadows enter the night.

And I recall now our twilight play
in the cemetery at the edge of town:
hide and seek among the gravestones
in the stone-eating dusk, the polished monuments
lacquered with a glowing phosphorescence.

The ground became a floating island, all shapes
drifting into the cool spanning dimming world—
our voices riding the old and passing breeze,
far away fell faint into the hills leaning into themselves.

In that slanting, waning light we lay flat
against the earth, hiding on the mounds of graves,
hunting ourselves in the dead city while crickets
told the old gossip of the world acre by acre,
closed the hinges of the sun's rusting minutes.

And all children equal with the dark country
coming on, we hid among those used-up names,
hollow letters engraved in stone as the hunter
stalked us, not knowing how later the hunter
would stalk us, not knowing when we called
alle alle oxen free how later we would learn
some are more free than others, some own power.

In a universe whose law is entropy, where
no power lasts longer than each day that dies,
what do children know who hunt each other
equally? Someone goes unarmed calling
our names, a stranger we once knew
wrapped in moonlight who walks between
all dreams, wearing the face of all children,
the face of all slaves who have scanned
the stars, wearing our own face and calling
alle alle auction free, everybody is also free,
home free, at home the night descends upon
the living and the dead the same.

Grandfather Schmidt

Moving outward is the fear.
Hands that know nothing except
to be hands, their language
the work they do, an argument
of blood against the sky.

If moonlight builds bridges above
the furious and falling rivers,
the earth by day still requires
struggle, the stubborn insistence
of a gardener, the hoe like
a crosier, the earth a place
to begin each dawn, coaxing
gladiolus to sell for funerals,
working the dark energies.

You, who fought the Kaiser
in World War I, knew a nation
was not the same as dignity,
the rich were not right, and said
you would not fight "in that dirty
god-damned war" in Vietnam,
not obedient to any king.

With your forehead where
winter wrote wrinkles,
your shoulders that supported
pillars on which mountains
were balanced, one night
the stillness became a fallen door:
a table where the grandchild
arrives to dine upon grief,
amazed at a world changed—
and what ancient strength
felled the door to pass like
thin darkness before the dawn.

For Tom McGrath

It would be something if
the enormous elm crashed
in the storm but its shadow
with all its dark foliage
silhouetted by the street lamp
remained against the house.

And when the wind rises
the shadow rears up,
a great spirit—its branches
reach toward the lattice
of lightning, and then:
the past, the shadow,
the house, tomorrow,
the stark fact of the world,
all revealed in a flash!

American Hitchhiking Blues

The train passes through the long hour of the prairie
while the dusty rasp of grasshoppers crackles
like kindling in the dry summer air, passes the small
country cemeteries, those ears closed to the century—
while distance climbs like Cézanne the cerulean
distance, the train tunnels into the horizon.

No ride for the hitchhiker far from home but
only the last hand luck skipping pebbles down
the concrete lane and the next city somewhere
between yesterday's dollar and tomorrow's change.
From the vantage of the train, if someone scanned
the country, the hitchhiker fades into the horizon.

And when distance shrinks to darkness, the homeless
know sidereal sadness in the back alleys, the chill
of those unsheltered under the hot far furnaces,
pinpricks of creation in cold remote time. Bums
and bag ladies wander the knuckle-gnawing night
while the moon somewhere else walks on water.

Autumn now. A few fallen leaves ripped out of summer.
The hitchhiker is long gone. The poor always happen
when the rest of America does not notice. And
the bones of Hart Crane, who believed in bridges
except across oceans, shift beneath wind and sea
while the dead stare through the bones of us all.

Rhoda Janzen

Dakota Road Trip

At small hotels
you flash your AAA
and gloat about décor

in harvest gold,
the slender packages
of wipes. Night

pulls a stranger's laugh
into the swamp-cooler.
You roll your sleeping

man back to his side.
Shadow wings his chin.
Somewhere a red

repeating wail orbits
unknown crime. Hours
bolt the romance down,

known but unfamiliar,
a faint and sphinx-like
figure. *You zipped me in*

your travel-size toiletries.
I am portable and personal,
I blue your bowl, I sanitize

the strip. Note what won't
suffice—ah, the driving
and the Tylenol it takes!

Let me remove the loving
little aches. Please answer
me, answer me, answer me.

Meux

Here is an antebellum house
made into a museum. The docent's
name is Mary. She is seventy,

a retired nurse, wearing the stiff
taffeta gown she bought for
a daughter's award ceremony,

a cartwheel hat with a brown
cabbage rose, her own mother's
shawl. Although the mansion is in

a seedy neighborhood, kids come
by the busload, and Mary does
her bit behind the velvet ropes.

She points out Margaret Meux's
receiver, the art that patient
Margaret made from tiny knots

of human hair. Here are owls
stuffed under glass, and General
Meux's old uniform, with

bloodspots on the sash. The General
didn't like it when little Missy's
friends came calling on a Saturday,

so before bed Missy tied a string
around her toe and threaded it out
the second story window, a silent

tug from friends whose daddies
likewise made their presence felt.
Here is a dish for calling cards

covered in gilt, and more owls.
To protect the deluxe damask divan
they shuttered the windows

right down to the sills. Mary, Missy,
Margaret, Meux. Walk out the doors.
There is nothing here for you.

Sonnet qui a fait quelques ajustements

The Grimm stepsisters hacked until they bled
dismemberment—possibly the very tale
with which Procrustes put his kids to bed.
In China, you could bind your lilies pale;

excision swaled the edge of the abyss,
navicular that hooved the three-inch cleft
so useful as a sexual orifice.
Phalanges curved beneath the sole, bereft

as widows on a weak annuity,
like little soured kumquats on the branch.
But don't believe the nothing that you see.
The flapper's chest, flat as an avalanche

and sudden as its absence, is so huge
that you could ride it whistling, like a luge.

The Edge

Picked and stemmed; trained
my thumb to blunt the knife,
pitting an aunt's concentration;

tucked sour cherries into sugar;
eked almond like a story, lapped
little pats of butter, pinch-cheeked;

sealed the scroll without tearing
the edge. Tart pink blush
on the pie-by-the-yard, long

like division for multitudes.
Pie-by-the-yard was heavy,
plump with the many moods

of guilt. Trust and obey
the edge, O church mouth!
When, amazed by grace, they

stood to sing, came the smell
of chins and casseroles, powdery
squeezes on the upper arm.

Mrs. Lorenz stooped, perfumed.
On her shoulder sat a phoenix
with a golden eye that bloomed

stern beneath the bluish perms.
No thank you, ma'am! Already
one of Harvey's summer storms

was darkening the plain.
Clouds crimped the sky. Now
distant thunder of a rolling pin.

North Dakota Sestina

(ending with a line from Psalm 19)

Beyond the matchbook parsonage
in fields reduced to stubble,
the rows untangled, as if a comb
had pulled them taut. The sigh
of the wind, sad at harvest, came rolling
like an old-fashioned wagon wheel.

The Liebelts' combine wheeled
around the tiny parsonage,
the great machinery rolling
toward the stiff August stubble.
Hulling loganberries, the child sighed
as she watched the combine comb

the wheat. Mornings, Mother's comb
straightened, thus: the braided wheel
of hair loosened like a sigh.
Racing from the tidy parsonage
to the fields of wild stubble,
the girl, hot, began rolling

her long sleeves. She tripped, rolling
down the incline into a catacomb
of indifferent yellow stubble,
sharp as the spokes of a wheel.
Her mother in the parsonage
came running. And the child sighed,

as if in all the Dakotas one full sigh
could stop the stupid tears rolling
or the thought of the stiff parsonage
and the terrible pull of the comb.
The mother rolled her like a wheel,
to see the scratches from the stubble,

but the girl saw only the stubble
collapsing in the field. She heard the sigh
of the combine finishing summer, the wheel
of winter like a thunderous silo rolling.
In her hair she spread her hand like a comb
and pinched her eyes shut to the parsonage.

Hair scythed short as stubble, she'd cartwheel
the parsonage and land in the field rolling,
a sigh sweeter than honey or the honeycomb.

Mark Vinz

The Doctor's Daughter

Come and get me
Don't forget me
Come and get me
Don't forget me
Come and get
This silly old lady

Today once again she talks in rhyme,
chants in rhyme, shouts in rhyme,
washed up from some far shore—those years
she was an elementary school teacher, perhaps,
or some childhood game more real
than this room with its unwatered plants,
its dusty family of framed photographs,
its padded wheelchair and hospital bed.

There was an old woman
Who lived in a shoe
She didn't know what
She should do, do, do

Upstairs and downstairs
In her nightgown
There is an old woman
Who runs through the town

Tell the others where I am, she says,
ever-cheerful smile beginning to crumble.
Where am I supposed to be? she says.
It's getting dark again, and who
will tell her where she needs to be?

Good night
Sleep tight
Bed bugs
Won't bite

In the early
Morning light

Child of a physician, she knows about
hospital beds and patients, all those times
she helped out in his office, all those visits
she made with him, just to keep him company,
sometimes with a horse and buggy to a farm
so far out in the sticks she thought they were lost,
singing together his favorite hymn.

> *This is my story*
> *This is my song*
> *Praising my Savior*
> *All the day long*

Don't you know how good it is to have a friend,
she says, to have the Lord there with you
all the day long and the long night too,
especially when there's nothing else to do?

> *And He walks with me*
> *And He talks with me*
> *And He tells me I am his own*

Her father used to walk with her sometimes—
the one who always stood up for her, even
when she sneaked out to have her hair bobbed
like some kind of Flapper, her mother said.

> *There was a little girl*
> *Who had a little curl*
> *Right in the middle of her forehead*
> *And when she was good*
> *She vas very, very good*
> *But when she was bad she was horrid*

It was her father who always indulged her,
except maybe that day at the lake when
he wouldn't let her try to land that lunker
she had hooked all by herself, which still tugs
on that line, doubling the pole, circling, diving,
just beneath the boat, until her father
takes the pole and slowly reels the monster in,
and even claims it, like it's *his* fish—
the one thing she can't seem to forgive him.

> *Come and get me,*
> *Don't forget me*
> *Treat me right*
> *And I won't fight*

Her mother, who once was a celebrity
in their small town, has receded into
the deepest shadows, off playing bridge
with her friends, off shopping, or simply
drinking coffee and gossiping, and now
there's just enough time to get dinner
in the oven, before her mother gets home.

> *Old Mother Hubbard*
> *Went to the cupboard*
>
> *Polly put the kettle on*
> *We'll all have tea*

Don't you know how she hates having to
do her mother's cooking and housework?
Don't you know she'd like to go somewhere, too,
maybe for a ride in her friend's new roadster,
back in the rumble seat with you-know-who,
not stuck watching her little brother
who can never keep from running off somewhere,
like the time they were visiting relatives
in some big city, and the only thing

that stopped him, that saved him, were all those
fascinating lights on a theater marquee,
a little like the county fair each summer.

> *Come and get me*
> *Don't forget me*
> *Come and take me to the fair*
> *Don't you know that I'll be happy there*

But there's no traveling now, no visiting,
no getting away. At the party for her
93rd birthday, the pile of cards keeps
appearing and then the cake and ice cream
and then the cards again and then the cake...

> *Little Bo Peep*
> *Lost her sheep*

> *Little Jack Horner*
> *Sits in the corner*

And now there are the ones who drool and smear
their food, the ones who coo, the ones who
always want to move her, and sometimes, too,
the one who rubs her back and holds her hand,
who might be husband or son or brother—
one of her favorite relatives.

> *Call, don't fall*
> *Is what the sign says*
> *Call, don't fall*
> *Call, don't fall*

Is it any wonder her voice is hoarse,
raspy, as she repeats her messages
          Come and get me
again and again, as loud as she can
          Don't forget me

eyes closed tight and chin thrust out
    Come and get me
head bobbing to the rhythm of the words
    Don't forget me

Who will tell her where she needs to be?
Who is going to come and take her hand?

The Last Time

for Tom McGrath

Your room, the nurse tells me,
is the one with the scanner in it—
that, and not to be afraid to wake you.
Most patients here sleep too much anyway.

You seem to know me at first,
when you ask for a beer and cigarette,
but then all light fades and you
shudder beneath blankets, clutching
at the tubes that grow from your arm.

What are you doing here? you say.
We'll miss the dance tonight.
And how about those fences that
need mending? Have to keep them out,
you know—all of them trying to get in.

What can I do? I keep asking,
beside the small red numbers forming
on the screen above your bed.
Old friend, we've finally reached the place
each road leads somewhere else.

I'll be gone for awhile, you say—
but you keep on watching as I
bend toward you, closer and closer,
farther and farther away.

Pioneer Village

One of those great grandmothers
I never knew was called Betsy—
my wife's name, too—
and in the county plat book
we've finally found her homestead site.
She didn't stay long, heading off
to California a hundred years ago.
Now, there's nothing else to mark her
in these acres of antiques,
buildings moved in from all over
the area—schoolhouse, church, and
drygoods store, even someone's jail.
Just another damned museum,
the man in the silly shark hat sighs.
He has to wonder what all this junk
could possibly be worth, his wife
busy photographing everything.
A map, some stories, a set of names—
Great Grandmother, Betsy,
Elverum Township, Pierce County,
North Dakota. Tell me, what's it worth?

North of North

Today with no surprise
the windchill sinks to 50 below.
The mailman slouches up the walk,
head down, the way we all learn how
to walk on this far edge.
You write to say how cold it must be here,
and thank whatever gods you have
this weather's north of you, far north.

But we say it too—
it's always colder somewhere else.
We praise our plows and furnaces,
fall back again on what we know:
there are no last words,
and what we speak of
is neither storm nor chill,
but what would happen if all letters stopped—
that other winter, directionless,
colder than ice, deeper than snow.

The Memory of Water

Here where the Sheyenne joins the Red—
upstream, the Bois de Sioux, and down,
the Buffalo—imagination finds its way
in swirls of white stirred by the prairie winds.

These are the places towns were built,
water flowing underneath snow-covered ice
laced with tracks of skis and snowmobiles
and creatures rarely glimpsed by passersby.

Today I'm home from a desert visit, where
two weeks of rain had finally broken—
arroyos carried everything away
except for the pools on asphalt roads.

How inevitably it all flows off and disappears—
water and what it has been named for—
here, in this glacial lakebed where I live,
still dreaming of the great herds passing.

Debra Marquart

Dylan's Lost Years

Somewhere between Hibbing
and New York, the red rust streets
of the iron range and the shipping yards
of the Atlantic, somewhere between

Zimmerman and Dylan was a pit stop
in Fargo, a superman-in-the-phone-booth
interlude, recalled by no one but
the Danforth Brothers who hired

the young musician, fresh in town
with his beat-up six string and his
small town twang, to play shake,
rattle, and roll, to play good golly,

along with Wayne on keys and Dirk
on the bass—two musical brothers
whom you might still find playing
the baby grand, happy hours

at the Southside Holiday Inn.
And if you slip the snifter a five,
Wayne might talk, between how high
the moon, and embraceable you, about

Dylan's lost years, about the Elvis sneer,
the James-Dean leather collar pulled
tight around his neck, about the late night
motorcycle rides, kicking over the city's

garbage cans, and how they finally
had to let him go, seeing how he was
more trouble than he was worth,
and with everyone in full agreement

that the new boy just could not sing.

Beating Up the Brother

Because he was a single stalk
of corn in a prairie of sisters,
because we girls were seven, nine,

eleven, and twelve, and he
was only ten—the middle one,
the fulcrum our farm turned on,

because he was too cute
and wore short pants. Little hand
in the cookie jar, little shrug

and grin. Because his buzz cut
felt like a freshly mowed lawn
when we drove our hands

over it, because Mom and Dad
left us alone some weekend nights
to watch Ed Sullivan and the Miss

America Pageant, because no beauty
from North Dakota ever won,
or advanced to the final round

of ten, because we were a gaggle
of girls, expected to fly away
and he would stay to plow

the land after we were gone,
because he was the only boy,
sweet-natured and forgiving

as Jesus under our fists, because
he was the brother, had that part
we thought of as extra, that part

we had never seen but knew existed.

Silos

ground zero   we believed
        we were   ground zero
                north dakota, 1964

minute men sleeping in silos   by the thousands
we knew   we couldn't say   we didn't know

ICBMs pockmarking the landscape
encased in concrete silos   six stories deep
buried in pastures
surrounded by cyclone wire
where holsteins muzzled through
for ungrazed grass

silos   bordering wheatfields
where farmers passed close by
with plows   seeders   combines
watched by soldiers
year round   in uniform   rifles in hand

small buried things   the great mirror underworld
grain silos above   missile silos below

        some people said they felt safer
        some said it helped the local economy
        some liked the men the missiles brought to town

there were launch command centers
disguised as family ranch houses
sprinkled around the countryside

        the basketball hoop above the garage door
        the radio tower on the roof
        the army jeep parked in the drive
        the chain-link fence around the perimeter

and below ground   deep concrete bunkers
where launch sequences were memorized
by the buried few   the survivors
          those who would avenge us
          at the ready   to strike   after we were obliterated

for decades   they memorized codes   protocols   launch sequences
          controlling the cluster of ten missiles each at their command

we knew   we couldn't say   we didn't know

but look around you   to the west   minot air force base
          to the east   grand forks air force base
                    how many air bases does one state need?

only the best get stationed up north, the airmen said
          what else could they say about drawing the short straw
                    the assignment in siberia   surely
                              they'd offended someone as powerful as stalin
                                        to be shipped here

strategically located   we were told
we were strategic   russia not as far away

as it might seem
one quick arc over the ice cap
north dakota to moscow

the shortest line between two points   they told us
          the small converging world
                    of the arctic circle

we knew   we couldn't say   we didn't know

ground zero   years later   we learned
          north dakota would have been the third largest
                    nuclear power in the world

   if we'd seceded from the union

Kablooey is the Sound You'll Hear

then plaster falling and the billow of gypsum
after your sister blows a hole in the ceiling
of your brother's bedroom with the shotgun
he left loaded and resting on his dresser.

It's Saturday, and the men are in the fields.
You and your sister are cleaning house
with your mother. Maybe your sister hates
cleaning that much, or maybe she's just

that thorough, but somehow she has lifted
the gun to dust it or dust under it (you are busy
mopping the stairs) and from the top landing
where you stand, you turn toward the sound

to see your sister cradling the smoking shotgun
in her surprised arms, like a beauty queen
clutching a bouquet of long-stemmed roses
after being pronounced the official winner.

Then the smell of burnt gunpowder
reaches you, dirty orange and sulfurous,
like spent fireworks, and through the veil
of smoke you see a hole smoldering

above her head, a halo of perforations
in the ceiling—the drywall blown clean
through insulation to naked joists, that dark
constellation where the buckshot spread.

The look on your sister's face is pure
shitfaced shock. You'd like to stop and
photograph it for blackmail or future
family stories but now you must focus

on the face of your mother, frozen at the base
of the stairs where she has rushed from
vacuuming or waxing, her frantic eyes
searching your face for some clue

about the extent of the catastrophe,
but it's like that heavy quicksand dream
where you can't move or speak,
so your mother scrambles up the steps

on all fours, rushes past you, to the room
where your sister has just now found her voice,
already screaming her story—*it just went off!
it just went off!*—as if a shotgun left to rest

on safety would rise and fire itself.
All this will be hashed and re-hashed around
the supper table, but what stays with you
all these years later, what you cannot forget,

is that moment when your mother
waited at the bottom of the steps
for a word from you, one word,
and all you could offer her was silence.

Somewhere in a House Where You are Not

There is sunlight coming through windows
somewhere in a house where you are not.

An old man and old woman eating breakfast
to the sound of the clock, out of words,

empty of thoughts, but for who died this year
and of what. If you follow the sun to that house

you will find the long lost driveway
that no highway intersects, the loose gravel

crackling under your wheels, the sun breaking
cleanly free of a horizon. You must park.

You must come to an absolute halt
outside the house where you are not,

letting your many necessary miles drop
from your bones like dust. Sit and wait.

Do not fear the mop-faced dog. He pounds
his tail for you. He is uninterested

in your tires. The old woman will soon come,
peeking through the ancient blinds, saying,

who on earth, and seeing your face
will hold out her hands, warm and soft

as good black dirt, and take you inside,
the house filling with your arrival,

the old man smiling his surprised skeleton smile,
the old woman asking, have you come far,

was it a long drive, are you hungry, are you
tired, to which you may answer, yes

and lie down in the bed they have kept
empty in your absence, reserved for the day

you would need this room full of nothing,
but rare morning light, and the stroke

of an old brown hand, inviting you
to rest, to sleep, to feel the earth

revolve slowly around and around
without you.

Robert King

Woman in the Home

Don't ask me why they built the Home on this side
of the town so we could sit all day and stare
back at the fields we used to work.

After my husband died, they found the paper
that left the land to the boy, the only thing
he ever wrote down in his life,

nothing of all the cash he'd given away
to the boy for gambling, ten miles down that road
you must have used to come out here.

My daughter got mad and left, and I was stuck,
a son for a husband, and a bad one too,
and me not knowing what I was.

He had worked to the end that day. First thing,
the mailman drives up, saying I better come,
some trouble in the corner field.

He'd stopped the tractor but hadn't shut it off
half down a row that went crooked behind him,
the engine roaring and waiting.

His heart just seized shut, they said, and what was strange
and made my own heart catch, his arms were propped up
beside his head, hands sticking straight

in the air as if he were surrendering.
I've thought on that a lot, figured I might go,
when the time comes, looking like that.

I don't think that corner field is ours by now.
If we were by the window I could show you.

Late Harvesting

Autumn, and the children leave,
night edging in from the roads.
The pickers rattle down the rows,
digging at whatever was buried:
potatoes, sugar beets, desire.
To reach the end is to return.

A wife rubs her eyes, slumps in the cab,
the conveyor throbbing against her.
Promises rise and pour into the bellies of trucks.
Her husband bends to pull at the world,
dredging the dirt for roots the shape of food,
their centers white as a daughter's skin.

All they held has loosened, emptied out.
In bed, exposed and numb, they open up into sleep
the way fields wait in the cold. Their hearts
echo, something pumping in the earth.

Trees bow, the shape of stones around the farm.
Sons are marrying in the black ditches,
daughters giving birth in the hollows of rooms, listening
to voices across the fields, their own childhood
calling from the porch in the first language.

Windbreaks

They liked the flat lay of the land,
nothing to stop the purpose of rows
or turn them back. The pioneer joke
was plowing a single furrow west
all morning, the second one home at night.

Now all our farms here have trees cutting
the fierce snow whipping across the fields
to carry them off an inch a day
or drift the house up to its windows.
Elm, cottonwood, Russian olive, spruce

smooth the wind, but I've found something else.
Farming is a matter of coming
and going. A year fills and empties
like my wife's each day, put down and pick up,
the fall fields clean as a kitchen floor.

We intend it all, and nothing stays.
The windbreak is an old relief from that.
In the center of that tree's a ring
for when I was born. Dead branches fall.
You let them lie. Leaves go soft with rot,

the dry grass melts, and the earth rises
as it deepens, keeping the loose hold
on time you need out of your control,
strips of richness rising around your life.

Fourth of July

Beyond the trees shadowing the farmyard
wheat seethes the color of the sun. The long day
shimmers across the fields, not a breath of breeze.
England is in a book we haven't read.
The land reaches too far to be called America.

Inside the shade we meet the young new wife,
the older ones, and talk about the winter,
quoting ourselves, ice melting around the beer
and watermelon in the galvanized tubs.
Here is a wheat field married to someone else.
Here is a divorce with two names. There
are the children, playing as if they belonged
to everyone, cousins named for the past.

The old ones sit almost beyond sight
in the dark parlor, chairs straight as their backs,
remembering a mother with red hair,
a husband who lost three farms in a lifetime.
One of them begins a story, it is an ocean,
it is before the ocean. The room is dreaming
the story, night in another country.
The voices tremble along old cobblestones.
Outside, the horseshoes clang like late church bells.

Behind the windbreaks to the west, the sun
boils down into a round red cloud and sinks.
Those of us left pull flimsy lawn chairs closer,
the song of our dim talk drifting the children
to sleep, games blurred into the rhyme of dreams.
Air is as warm as the blood. The summer family thickens.
The fields widen around us, dark as a huge room.

The Shape of the World

Waves lap the snowy fields outside our house, each furrow
the rib of a dune, the ripples of a creek bed
in white stone, curves of the landscape's repetitions.

Last autumn we walked in the low round hills,
bare trees like the maps of rivers pouring back
into the earth, each leaf the print of a stream

within its latticework of creeks. We found ourselves
wandering inside the valleys of our hands.
We turn now like the last people, reaching out.

The old wind rubs, cornering the house, and we are trees
dancing with each other against the air.
The red seaweed of our nerves stretches and divides

into the finest of complications as winter, cutting
and smoothing around our delicate intentions,
blows over and over into the shape of the world.

Aaron Poochigian

Captain Lewis at the Pacific

We toed the ocean, so the time had come.
Seagulls were seagulls. It was afternoon.
We had to head back where we started from.

Great men would praise me from the podium
just as they cheered, years back, a Daniel Boone
so broken to the ways of heathendom
that he ate dog and fumbled with a spoon.

There was the East but, when I would have swum
for Shanghai, fought even the wild monsoon,
duty deterred me from delirium.

Back home I hope to drop whatever sum
my field notes fetched me on an air balloon
and sail off, with a basket full of rum,
for El Dorado, maybe, or the moon.

Grand Forks, ND

To make it back home for the holidays,
Interstate Twenty-nine, a black ice glaze:
the smokestacks at the Crystal Sugar Plant
spouting the only mountains, tumbledown
slaughterhouses, barns sagging aslant,
and homesteads under heaps like winter wheat—
scant signs of life, and, goddamn, several feet
of fresh obscurity have blurred the town.

What now? The Mustang hung up in a ditch,
there's no choice but an outside world in which
hinged things are creaking—car doors, elbows, knees.
But all is calm now that the wind has fallen.
Time slows down as in epiphanies.
Breath swirls and swirls away. I had forgotten
snowflakes could float about like this, like cotton
from cottonwoods, like tufts of crystal pollen.

Stock and Bond

Since the recession my domestic
dream has been one bedroom, one bath,
a porch, a hammock and a path
cutting through weeds to the majestic
remnants of a Cadillac,
an ax stuck in a chopping block
and, further out, a rickety dock
where the companions I throw back
are always waiting to be fed—
gilded and silvered, carved from jade,
the whole fortune I never made,
shimmering in a pond, instead.

Mrs. Pulaski's Shrine

Despite the drainpipe daily
bringing up bolder roaches,
and the imbalanced couches,
dragged in from the alley,
breeding mites and mice,
this shack is sacred space:

a doily marks the holy
of holies, and vase
magnifies the lace,
and lilies-of-the-valley
from out of this world perfume
the one room, the whole home,

the whole soul of the place.

Our Town

Like houselights dimming in a theater,
the sunset was a signal: drama would occur.
Street lamps here and there
spotlit familiar objects in the square—
some benches, a swing set—as if they were
of consequence. The sprinklers hushed on cue.
Where was the *jeune premier*, the aproned ingénue?
Would they appear and air
big dreams, grand schemes, the regional despair?
No, not this evening. They had chores to do.

Reluctance like a curtain coming down
smothered the lark, and there it was, our town
again, a blip vanishing into prairie,
and no roads leading to the luminary
metropolis where life was all night long
drinking and dancing, bursting into song.

Heidi Czerwiec

Song Against Songs

You were singing. I was listening
full of dark water. Your song was waiting,
a small, hard green, but false spring was blooming
after the last sky. Against songs,

false spring was listening, a small, hard green.
I was against songs. Your song was blooming
after the last sky. Full of dark water
you were singing but waiting.

Song against songs. But false spring
was blooming, a small, hard green after the last sky,
full of dark water. Against songs, listening:
a small song, hard, but green. You were singing to me.

Fall Rondeau

It's fall. I'm knitting pairs of winter socks
and trying not to see the veeing flocks
fleeing South. Traitors. It's not cold
yet. The locals have just begun to fold
away the lawn chairs, to pull up the docks.

Instead of raking, or taking rambling walks
I sit outside, stitch and purl the sumac's
flaming red, the elm's glowing gold.
It's fall I'm knitting

into these socks. My Southern blood balks
at the Midwestern winter coming. It stalks
my every thought. And yet, each sock that's rolled
off my needles staves off winter's toehold.
It's fall. I'm knitting.

Cardinal Directions: Divorce Fugue

Grand Forks, 2004

December brought you to this place, this air
full of frozen embers of itself.
What you're looking for is cardinal.
There will always be, the poet claimed,
such things that you regret knowing.
For *you* read *I*. Any way you go
will be far, each breath a scrape like splintered bone
against the windpipe. Listen: the crows alone
brave winter's hands. All other birds seek shelter.

Any way you go from here is far.
Thou hast doves' eyes in thy locks.
I kept listening: the crows black blots
perched on winter's gloves. There will always be things
you know. (For *you* read *you*.) The swoop and fall
of cries that fill the Carolina foothills,
trees full of birds like red clots
(What you're looking for is *cardinal*.)
A__ followed me to Utah but no farther.

Listen: the crows (*Corvus brachyrhyncos*)
interrogated winter's too-many hands.
There will always be such things that you
regret knowing. In this place, only space is grand.
December left you cold—you went forth,
fleeing like you've fled all places North.
I took shelter in birdwatching, tried not to think of you
(for *you* read *A__*), or of how any way
I tried to go from here would be far.

Thou hast doves' eyes within thy locks.
You keep listening for familiar birds
among winter's singularity of crows.
There will always be such things that you regret.

What I'm looking for is cardinal
direction, a song, a sin that won't
omit me, absolution from being unloved.
A__'s love did not extend to places North—
it followed me to Utah, then no farther.

Fault. Lines.

Incline Fault, Salt Lake City

Next to your house the ground has slipped
away, a dip that divides you

from next door by forty vertical feet. You sensed
the rift growing. You were not

inclined to notice. In faulty
logic there is slippage between two planes

of thought. Between two people. How ice
sends cars slipping

against steep curbs. How any day now, geologically speaking,
the Big One could hit. When it does,

when it all slips away, when he
slips away, first there will be heat, then some form of stasis,

however askew. The divorce decree will read *no-fault*.
And though you think you can't

you will climb and cross
two continental divides, the miles

slipping away beneath your car
until you come to a place lacking topography,

its absence of altitude palpable which is to say
without fault, slippage here only
horizontal, in a place only horizon.

Sedating the Cats

Each morning they hid, the drug's tuna taste
fooling no one. *It'll make the move easier,*

I said, pinning them myself, because *They like you
better than me*, he said. Soon they'd stagger

like drunks, meows thick in their mouths,
inner eyelids drifting back and forth

uncontrollably across their sight. I draped
their carrier against the cold with a blanket.

Also to calm them, as one would
a horse or parrot. Despite my deceptions,

each night they'd pin down my limbs,
kneading me with their nearness—

their weight not the same as his weight
in a different bed, in the same room.

Each morning the drug and me
crying until I couldn't see straight.

Once, we slid off the icy road. Then even
their slurred murmuring went silent. I was shaking

uncontrollably—from shock, from subzero cold. The man
who accompanied me was the same man

who would abandon me once we arrived.
Each morning, the drug. Each morning,

me wishing for something to make it easier.
When we arrived, they hid from me for a week.

Tim Murphy

Travels with Chucky

I. *Wrong Game*

Chucky is really into hunting voles.
They poke their beady eyes from tunneled holes
    and scurry through the grass
    where black retrievers pass,
and they are field snacks which my puppy rolls.

Pheasants, he hasn't figured out, not yet,
nor ducks, these are game he has yet to vet;
    the puppy's after mice
    he gobbles in a trice,
then throws up in my lap. Precocious pet.

II. *Passing the Torch*

He pointed his first pheasant, then he pounced.
It crashed into a shaven soybean field
but took off running; and the puppy trounced
our target with a passion labs can wield,
full somersault on impact in his glee,
then fetched his flapping trophy to my knee.

Two years ago I wrote a poem here.
I had a winged bird twenty feet away
from Puppy's flush. Though young dogs rummaged near,
old Betty nailed him. That was her last great day
before the cancer. Now my eyes well up.
I watched her somersaulting as a pup.

III. *The Risks of Unloading*

The tailgate of my little Ford Escape
stands five feet ten. I've grazed it, only once.
I'm tall enough it gave my scalp a scrape,
but Steve collided with it. Autumn hunts
rarely end with a hunter streaming blood,
only with boots clotted by prairie mud.

The camper on Steve's F-150 Ford
towers so high I sometimes have to leap
to latch its panel. From a ditch I've soared
(I'd never do this with a middling Jeep
or with my small Ford Motor SUV).
Norwegians are our climax prairie tree.

Stevie, who's taller than my truck is wide,
fell to the asphalt with a whimpered groan.
I pulled my puppy from our hero's side,
latching him in the kennel with a bone,
then whistled *Morgenstimmung* in Stevie's ear
until his blue eyes opened to the blear

sight of a tailgate high above his head.
Only the ducks, not my dear friend, were dead.

IV. *Chucky's First Snow*

The steps are icy where the garden hose
leaks, and the ice is strewn with windblown snows.
Ass over tea kettle, my puppy goes
plummeting down the stairs, his landing soft.
I laugh at him, my vantage high aloft,
near six feet to his two. The west winds waft
over my black-fur-coated ball of lard
their short-lived snowflakes. Across the drifted yard
where Puppy rolls, his gunner stands on guard.
My falls and landings? Most of them have been hard.

V. *West River Chucky*

Hunters: most are the have-nots, few, the haves.
It's not the birds. It's dogs. Flush and retrieve.
In cattails you are bouncing off my calves.
As I believe in God, you must believe
your nose, learn to quarter ahead of me.
Maggie has three birds, you precisely zero.
Follow her through the slough, the CRP,
and Puppy, someday you will be my hero,
tracking my winged birds through the snow, the grass,
ferreting out the furtive from the trees
dropping their last leaves, foils of polished brass.
You'll fetch wild roosters to your master's knees
which now, Bad Puppy, you attempt to climb.
We've world enough, and we're on Mountain Time.

Ed Bok Lee

Year of the Dog

hot in the year of the dog, i sip whiskey and coke on my rooftop; sparrows weaving together this summer evening full of nothing but two shirtless Mexicans, my neighbors, mustached Elvises in the twilight, who once took a chicken apart with gloves of blood and feathers, and now pick-ax a gravel echo deep in the back alley of this immigrant tale leading to dust and broken bottles

one of them, wiping away the sun's last rays from his forehead, looks up and stares at the heart within the cough of his sweaty son, or brother, cousin, fellow man

they come, i know, for their children, these two Ezekiels of daily-dishwashed hands and fry-pocked countenance; come for their women, raven-maned Marias hanging damp tube socks, stained workshirts, and pajama tops from branches and chain link; come like anyone to this neighborhood from Mexico, Sudan, the hills of Laos and Tien Shen Mountains, packed at the backs of night banana trucks, faceless, alien-eyed ghosts in border patrol heat-sensing photos, stuffed in shrimp trawlers and gassy trunks of cars, each day negotiating a border of stars, hauling summer nights and salty dreams, lit by Bics and stooped by the moon on their backs. come because God intoned they'd otherwise end up like him, on a fishhook in the sea

only to arrive late every night like my mother, who places her cast-iron rice cooker of twenty years on the curb. through the window i watch not her stoop and limp, but the dilapidated slippers which carry her to this far end of the world; helpless slippers i once hid, but long to eat now from the garbage of my dreams

visions, incantations so slippery tonight, in hands clinking dishes, turning bolts; listen closely how they chop, slice, zip, sew, push, pull, tug, bend, but never ever break; see their swollen factory feet years underneath eyes bleary on Sunday evenings at the Target on Lake Street, four minutes before closing, an entire Somali family parts the doors like a sea of glass, Mother cloaked in blue tunic and hijab, Father in flip-flops, five young children inside; the smallest of them stops and stares back at me through

Mohammedan angel eyes, holding a potted cactus and Koran, as if challenging me to remember his fate. is he our hero at age seven, or the villain?

come for your job, your home, your daughter's uterus, your son's soul; the laundromat your family built up and protected with bullets of sweat, only to watch it torn down by similar fingers clutching torches and shopping carts loaded down with beef and stereo equipment, rioting through an evaporated Lake Agassiz like locusts come, killer bees, gypsy moths you can't see stealing fruit in their infinitesimal hands, tax dollars, unemployment; come to ESL classes, stretching verbs and adjectives to place their plucked tongues back on mango trees, chestnut, rambutan; stumbling through burning jungle brush and a heaven of metal detectors, skipping over a dozen words for water; a scale of scars from para-military raids in the dark, tattoos sun- and wind-carved like mishealed wing joints, fleeing fourteen year old soldiers wielding hacksaws across scorched savanna

only to end up in Fargo, Rochester, Wabasha, Sioux Falls, humming along to the pitch and fall of a snowy drift alone in a borrowed bedroom; refugees from Bosnia and Saigon, come to till the abandoned prairies, ghost towns of a century and a half ago, where Swedish songs of sugar beet farmers still mist the one-room church house windows

if you concentrate, you can still hear their wails in the wind; journey the spine of abandoned railroads on the Dakota Plains to the end of civilization past vagrant, shot-through Indian reservations, and you know how they came, but where did they go?

these guardians of the night's floating soul; these aching knees, palms and fingernails hauling ten generations of shadow and soil

this family living next door in the twilight...

who used to be my own.

On the Velocity of Souls

Old souls tend
to gravitate toward cities,

dull coins, museums.
Wanting to sense more

waning power.
New souls prefer

bucolic landscapes:
lakes, manageable

woods, suburbs.
Of course, both new and old

souls will one day cross paths
like a changing of the guards,

maybe even nod, trading
news of ice ages, rain forests-

cum-deserts, a recent
heinous crime.

Plagues, jokes, undying
lovers, genocides.

Though never true friends,
old and new souls, they

respect each other. Unless
one is still angry

at the judgment the other
passed eons ago—

Pay heed: whoever you are
will be, and

were.

Mrs. Joseph B—On Love, Sin, & Celadon

When he came home from the war
we didn't sleep together for four months. He put
a sprinkler system in, ceiling moldings, chain-
sawed branches. I was touching myself

on the toilet and my daughter walked in. I grounded her
for mimicking the noises over dinner cabbage rolls.
How do you come back from that:
however many breaths like birds it torments him

he took from those people. He'd disappear
some evenings, so I picked up pottery and extra hours
at the travel agency. A man, a client, asked me to happy hour.
It was dark at 4:35; the snow airy wet, hypnotic.

We went to his condo after shrimp toast and I wanted to swallow
the ring in my purse. His wife, he said, had lesbian
inclinations he'd ignored at first. I listened to him,
his suffering over such preventable things, which, in a way,

is greater suffering like a toothache versus soulless soul. He smelled
like smoke and cinnamon cologne and I thought he might be the Devil.
Still I went to him often. Did my husband even care?
I couldn't believe in ghosts, dead or living.

When I bloated with the other man's child, I confessed all.
My daughter screamed and wept; slammed the back door.
She called me slut, a traitor, and howled from the yard
how could I with a *the N-word*. I told her we're all human.

My husband didn't fight. We prayed and I killed my baby
at the same place I picketed with my Small Group
when I was my daughter's age. Sacrifice. An eye
for an eye. My husband killed

somewhere far away, and so did I, right here.
I knew it wouldn't resurrect his casualties. But I swear,
when seated each week with him hand in hand
in that fluorescent waiting room at the V.A.,

I understand his fear and longing to return to the desert.
He's a good man, and so wants to die.
It's why I married him.
And, now, why I must help him change.

Neon Pyramid

"The real war will never get in books."
          —Walt Whitman

Once upon a time, I bagged cowboys with a tomahawk

Now in this cold casino on a rez past midnight
                                        I too am shot
by smug expressions of Native pit bosses
at every player ready to leap chipless off a cliff

After all, why expect any sympathy for a Korean,
Black, Mexican, Somali, Lebanese—clung detritus
in the flood of passing faces on their secret video screens—who, granted,
never foraged in with beads, bullets, smallpox, & dummy contracts,
but nevertheless:

Slam dust off green felt
Curse their dealers
Snort speed in the bathrooms
Mis-cardcount with rusty brains
Always celebrating too quickly

Hard to blame them

No one expects a body's organs to float you this far
into prairie hinterland from Midwestern
common sense
                              But tonight the heart
is a drunken, belligerent bus driver—
                                        Cordoned off
in High Stakes mid-July, stranded
by wars & lost marriages, layoffs, cost of power
& gas, businesses
                              belly-up, or just retired low-
fat boredom & a life played equally bad

                                        Sometimes they speak,
a player's shadow language: massaging
past lives furrowed in brows—

I Iran & hate both a Arab & the Jew

Luck is a river's fishes

Hey, my cleavage is the happy cadaver of a famous bank robber!

Tolstoy, you ragged, onion-reeking Cossack, what
would you minister to these fellow congregants
in this last resort anti-church? I've seen you

dragging your oxygen tank to & from the Wild Sevens slot island
three nights in a row before they stretchered you out
unconscious in the same clothes
                                        Is God really dead,
or the killer capitalistic streak, this flashing jackpot, that behemoth
bingo payout turning wrists & retinas to stone?

Fortunately, tonight it doesn't matter, because
Dostoevsky, broken addict extraordinaire, is here
third shift, Windexing mirrored pillars, scanning
the carpet for butts & a stray
chip every several years
                                        Little Father, what wisdom
have you for me tonight other than to drink
my bitter milk & stand up straight
or else?
            All I wanted was ease
from boiling dreams, & now
the self-same thirty-two pop song loop
has satellite-beamed into our wheezing;
the entire kingdom at a toxic symbiosis—
                                        Desperation re-circulating cool desire

The Buddhist to my right bets table max then stands,
all four-feet six—a sugar beet farmer who'd eat your car

to survive; whose circular, chain-smoking stories resemble
a Shanghai river at dawn

Or take the cowgirl cursing in Spanish to my left, surely a heart
of amber with that eyeliner, accompanied by rotating
twenty-something white men to bear witness & light her menthols—big sister
to regret, busty grandmother to shame, in black knee-high boots, maybe
once a prostitute, but now just a solid third-base table mate;
greedy, but at least consistent in her hits & stays,
attuned to the rhythm of our four-deck like a drum machine

Tonight, no open seat for loneliness

As long as you play,
announces this Cleopatra cardslinger with the prettiest flow of turquoise nails
Did we just trade retorts & hand signals as if bathing spirits
two hours & only once did our knuckles
kiss?
              Or were we laughing at each other's angels?

Because I am dying
                    to know what will become of all this hope

Can the heart decay waiting?

Or like the somber Crip with a queen diamond
& six spade tattooed on his neck, his plaintive chant:
every minute is a worse possible hand—
                              Will it too slink
away its aging display of faded images?
Or sit here forever
                    sipping bright-green anger?

Past 4 a.m., every face a refugee of human features
                                        And I know:
you can't win the past
                    or stalk redemption

But neither does death get any cheaper

Like the young mechanic
who hit the Super Bond 007 jackpot,
but wasn't of legal age to collect—
                                        Come back

the next night, a sawed-off shotgun
stroking his thigh
                        Or so everyone loves to tell

The point: anyone could win big at any time!
Most will crawl back into their shells
& sputter home
                        Others will die
dreaming of free liquor & smoke
Mortgages, partnerships, retirements—in a cloud

Some, like this fake-baked pregnant girl
even joke-threaten she'll call the FBI
for fraud
                as she hits
                                & her mascara soon melts

But none at this hour will hand over fear
                                        without a fight

All I have
                is my life

The Schooner

Farther inside this long bar near Lake and Hiawatha, they burn
Over beers in the dark, these men and two women, creaking
Fatigue on stools, dead drunk. It is summer. The sun a cancer.
The God of Silence today has called a quorum of minor gods who have created
And destroyed whole voices and lives. Where else to go
If all you want is to drink to the sound of clearing throats?

The verdict is in. Men of Hope shall be resigned to steal quiet turns vomiting.
Stunned prairie horse spirits surviving civilization.
Some come with money to grin through a second happy hour.
Others doze after one shot like a bullet from behind. Teetering
Faded tattoos over silver threads of drool. The bartender
Collects a pile of quarters and dimes, picks out the lint.
Sally, an old white lady with a pink mohawk, cackles. Sometimes
Life splatters like an artist with no training or vision.

*

Imagine stick figures walking through a world of rich, seeping colors.
Smiling, they inhabit donated, baggy denim and flannel. One fermenting soul gets stabbed
For singing another's karaoke song. One human being in red sparkly pumps
Gets attacked then imprisoned for being too male or female for another's liking.
Meth once in the popcorn machine. Pull tabs rigged. Meat raffle rigged.
Every bar at 2 pm is a ship just after the storm.
You're alive is enough cause for celebration!

**

I could tell you I drank there because
The attic I lived in had no air-conditioner. I could say
It was a period when I was unemployed; or lived only two blocks away; my father took his life;
I just liked fruit flies. I remember a novel-in-progress about space garbage.
And on the 4ᵗʰ of July and Super Sunday, they put out celery and pizzas for free
On the duct-taped pinball machine.

But, really, it was the *water lilies*—how they'd reappear and disappear
In the stiff, late-night breeze, buzzing
Above crushed cans and condoms in wet leaves, on each slow stumble home.
One, a fuzzy planet. Another, a troubled century.
A third, just a lazy-eyed junkie on the block named LeNay.

* * *

A man steps into a bar, takes a seat between an old Norwegian, a Somali,
And an Indian. There is no punch line.
Instead, it's like anti-church. Or descending the Grand Canyon.
Only at bedrock, can you look up
And witness all the lavish gradations of loss. The world
Is full of missionaries. Only the Angel of Death
Can kiss and hand you the knife
You'll need to carve out your own capacity to be happy.

So I did.

Denise Lajimodiere

His Feathers were Chains

After William Stafford

At a small town in South Dakota
I stopped to rest
and saw an Indian on a horse
welded together using farm implements
and planted on the lawn next to the Chief motel.

His war bonnet was a sickle bar,
his shield a disc blade,
his feathers were chains,
a splicer connector formed

his mouth into a permanent oval,
his horse's body was a barrel,
a harrow for a tail,
his hoofs support brackets.

I found him there
and heard a war cry from his mouth
like howls in my chest.
Is one a warrior only when reveille is heard?
Forgive me friend, but he was there

at Wounded Knee, Little Big Horn,
Washita, Sand Creek, Whitestone Hill,
and has a harrowing tale to tell
staked to this earth,
his blood a rusty red.

String Too Short to Use

for Carol Davis

In winter we butchered a pig, placed in a tub,
and stored on top the cabin; we rendered fat
from pork, pounded cream to butter, lowered
in the well, cooling with the eggs;

caught gophers and roasted them on a spit, eaten
with raw or roasted *navoos*. Venison sliced
in strips we hung by the stove to dry, then stored
in calico bags with peppermint to keep

the ants at bay. Uncles hunted rabbits,
skinned and boiled to make a *rubbaboo*.
Grandpa trapped muskrats in spring, boiled,
them up added potatoes and wild onions,

turnips or *esquibois,* poured in cast
iron kettle and put into the oven.
For a special treat we roasted muskrat tails
on top the old wood stove or stuck in camp

fire embers, stripped the skin, enjoyed.
We ate the older hens for Sunday supper,
killed a skunk before he sprayed, then took
his oil, bottled and stored it in a medicine

room, used it for pneumonia and flu;
went with Kookum early mornings before
the spirits woke to gather plants and roots
for medicine, hung them upside down

on cabin beams. We gathered wild hops
on banks of creeks to use as yeast in dough,
pulled sweet cattails from the slough,
aunties danced to loosen the mud around

the roots we used as leavening for bread.
Stored half the vegetables from the garden
in a cellar under the floor, the other half
fit into a six foot pit outside, then set

a door over the vegetables, hay
on top the board, and sealed with rich black dirt.
Uncle Joe traveled to Elbow Woods
to trade oak posts and berries for Hidatsa

sisters, corn, beans, pumpkins, and squash,
canned the rest to have a taste of summer
when forty below; Kookum pounded chokecherries
on rocks, shaped them into cookies and dried

on top the roof, a screen to fool the crows,
reconstituted the cookies at Christmas with water,
bacon grease, sugar and some flour,
fried in cast iron skillet on the stove.

For breakfast we ate leftovers from supper,
ate anything not considered a rodent,
or crawling on the ground. In summer we carried
the old wood stove outside, and placed it under

the cool shade of aspen tree boughs.
Mother made syrup from brown sugar and coffee,
bacon grease was used in oatmeal and anything
else we wanted to pour it over, including

our hair, which made it shine like a beaver's pelt.
We had running water, ran down the hill
to the slough and fetched it, hauled it back
to wash our clothes, even in the winter

hung outside, frozen stiff and flat.
On cold winter nights a three boiled tea was made
by melting snow in a corn syrup pail, skimming
rabbit 'beads' that floated to the top,

when water boiled threw a handful of leaves,
removed it from the fire, then boiled again,
three times it boiled, we drank without sugar,
because we usually didn't have any by then.

Stormy winter evenings we sat around
the stove eating pukkons, picked in the fall,
and stored on top the lean-to roof. We listened
to stories of *tawn kiyash,* buffalo hunts,

battles with *nadousisioux,* and Kookum's
sarsaparilla would be passed around,
she stashed her money in Bag Balm cans, buried
them somewhere in the bush under a birch tree,

made quilts from grandpa's Bull Durham tobacco
bags with army blanket batting. Stored
in blue glass jars with lids were buttons and ribbon,
made dresses sewn from floral flour sacks,

and sequined moccasins from army canvas,
Aunt Mary braided old brown socks into rugs,
cut Ojibwe floral designs from wool
material, embroidered onto rugs.

Mops were cut from old dress shirts and rags,
curled our hair with rags or wrapped brown paper
around tin strips cut from Prince Albert tobacco cans,
rolled up our hair and crimped the curls in.

Plastic curtains worked just fine, susurrus
in the summer breeze. Sheer curtains from
the bundles used as netting over cribs.
The heart of a stump so old the center had turned

to a powder so fine could be used as talcum.
Newspapers and gift wrappings made festive wall paper,
put tissues that wrapped apples and oranges
in bloomer drawers as potpourri, the lovely

scented tissue from peaches went straight to the outhouse.
Dad kept crooked nails hammered them straight;
he flattened tin cans to shingle the chicken coop.
I wore the same dress to school for a week,

shared clothes with sisters and cousins. Not to waste
water, we took a bath on Sunday nights,
tried not to be the last one in the tub.
When out of kerosene ma put sugar

in a rag, twisted it tight, soaked
in grease and lit, or cut the tab from baby's
shirt, the part that pinned it to the diaper, broke
out the inside of a button, and slid

the tab on through then placed the button on
the side of a bowl of grease, used this little
lamp until we could afford kerosene.
Last, hugs were saved for those we loved.

Dakota January

The moon of bone cracking cold,
of Styrofoam crunch snow,
The snow blind moon
The moon of white outs,
short days, long nights,
The moon of blizzards,
of popping tree limbs,
The moon of thirty days below zero,
of wind chill advisories,
frostbit, blackened skin,
The moon of frozen lakes,
The least heat moon,
The moon of white suns,
communion discs,
The Alberta clippers moon.

Kiwetin blasts from the north,
howling a frigid refrain.
Diamond dust ice crystal dogs cup
the sun's brilliant face
resting on a pillar,
a second set, a pale mirage
reflected in frozen snow,
polished to a high shine.
Snow rivers flow across
the plains, toward
a pale horizon.
Kiwetin roars and I'm surrounded
by a circle of ghost buffalo,
warmed by their breath.

Slow Time

She rises to stoke the old Monarch stove,
her place in the bush more a cabin than a house,
puts a pan of water on so I can wash my face
and get dressed then head out to school
where I'll teach fourth graders reading and times
tables. She puts on her calico dress and well-worn

apron sewn from torn clothes others have worn.
She will busy herself about the stove
getting ready for lunch time.
Chops wood, stacks it by the house,
and waits my return from school,
combs her hair, puts *la-rouge* on her face,
pins her curls and she's ready to face
the day, same as before, rutted and worn
as the reservation road I take to school.
She sits on her couch, away from the stove,
listens to quiet of her house,
shuffles cards and thinks about old times.

The wringer washer needs filling, hard time
carrying water from nearby slough, facing
an uphill climb winding back to the house
through trees, leaves ticking, the path well worn.
To boil water she puts more wood into the stove.
The cool steam greets me when I return from school.

I help hang clothes on the line as the school
bus rattles by kids waving. When it's supper time
she brings in a load of wood and feeds the stove,
makes *rubbaboo* and fry bread. I feed my face
while she puts her tea kettle on the stove. Worn
out from work inside and outside the house,

and thinking of days gone by, she houses
many memories, wishes she had gone to school
past the third grade. Sitting in the worn
corner of her couch, she calls evenings 'slow time,'
shuffles her cards that no longer have faces,
while boiling drops dance like tears on the hot black stove.

We listen to the snaps in the stove,
as the house cools she schools
her cards, faces disappeared, shuffling, shuffling, worn.

My Grandfather was a New Initiate

My grandfather was a new initiate
at the Ft. Totten Indian boarding school.
He was told he had to steal a can of tomatoes,
a sweet fruit to these hungry little boys in the dorm.

Down the cement stairs,
past the headmaster's studio
with its own bath,
into the Dakota dark
he stumbled across Cavalry Square
to the outside kitchen shed door,
fumbled for the hanging string,
down the narrow stairs,
grabbed the heavy can and lit
out into the steel arm of the headmaster.

They brought me to the magazine room
where a barrel was strung across.
I had to lay over it and two bigger boys held my arms.
The little boys had to watch.
The headmaster whipped my bare back with a rubber hose.
Uh, uh! I couldn't breathe,
couldn't catch my breath.
I passed out.
The boys said they had to hold me up for one more whip.

At Ft. Totten today
red bricks crumble
beneath white paint.
Name plaques on the buildings
recognize its days as a fort
and then a boarding school.
Standing inside the magazine/flour storage room,
it's small,
maybe ten by ten.
How did all the little boys fit?

As I stood and wept,
the hot July winds
gathered forces from across the plains
and hurled like warriors
into the square,
an arrow soaked in gunpowder,
lit, aimed and the room exploded around
me, the bricks a liquid red.

Jamie Parsley

These Men

All the men of this family
die the same way.
After years of heavy labor
they take to their beds
in their exhaustion
and never rise again
from that grasping last sleep.

In that endless night
their arteries tighten and close up.
The pulse slows and stops.
In that dawnless time
their hearts malfunction
like clogged carburetors
shutting down.

For others, labor was a curse.
But for these men
they frowned every time
they heard the pastor speak of Adam
being cursed to work the earth.
Is it a curse? they wondered.
Or is it grace
to rise early in the morning
and to go to the earth
to work? It was, rather, benediction.
What they brought home on their hands—
those deep-creased fingers
stained with crude oil
and petroleum grease
and dirt—
was unction.
It was the chrism they
anointed themselves—
and us—
with.

The Gathering

The ghosts of the trees he felled
gather here

at this place we set him,
their shadows swaying and leaning

toward this footspace of earth,
blotting its details in the grass,

its earthen lines,
still fresh and disturbed

as a not-yet healed surgical scar.
You stand with them—

you who never toppled a tree
nor even stripped bark from

those sentries who stand guard here.
How like them you are

in this cold, late
afternoon moment.

How tall you stand—
how straight and firm.

Two

after a poem by K.N. (Kristjan N. Julius, 1860-1936), Icelandic-
born American poet, buried at Thingvala Lutheran Church near
Mountain, North Dakota.

I depend upon the moon—
the moon, that moon.
It's never failed me—

not once in all these years
that have gone on in my life,
through endless nights like this one.

How many times have I—
lost and groping about in the dark—
found the path it casts its light upon

in the dark
and found my way back?
In the deep blue,

it has stared back—
pale as a saint's face.
Fractured, it will soon

be full. And then,
in that deep silence,
it will, as it always has,

wait for me.

* * *

"I don't even know where my own grave is"
          —James Wright

I know where mine is. It is there
this evening under a blue
shadow of spackled snow.
The moon falls lightly there
where everything lies undisturbed
except for the haphazard tracks
of sparrows and jackrabbits.

I have obsessed about
this square of earth, now frozen
down a good several feet, beneath
wind-sheened snow.
I have dreamed of it
in fevered nights which
never seemed to end
and took refuge there
when my days sunk into
seemingly eternal encroaching dusks.

Everywhere I have gone
I have always come back
to that cool clean place,
its very ground formed
to receive not the arrogant violation
of a backhoe and the persistent rust
of funereal metals,
but the simple disposition
of whatever remains
following the dawn-like
glow of the fire.

Ghostly

"...in knowing of God and of ghostly things..."
    —Walter Hilton

Ghosts always obsessed me,
not vampires or ghouls or werewolves.
Ghosts, unlike other fictions,
seemed more plausible. Ephemeral shapes
and faces, like all our dead,
seemed possible
and in those long dark nights
I could almost hear them,
wandering about, sighing sadly
in the hallway or shuffling around the corner.

Ghosts *could* be real I thought.
Death, after all, was a reality for me,
and because it was,
I hoped, in my way, that it was more
than just a mysterious all-encompassing darkness
we braced ourselves against
when we paused long enough
to consider it.

I hoped
even before religious belief piqued
that somehow we went some *where,*
that we went on in some *way*—
it didn't matter how,
just as long as we didn't stop being,
curled up into a nihilism
that seemed more tragic
than anything else I could imagine.

I believed that they—
the ones who had gone into that strange, murky place,
that foggy other-world—
knew us and saw us,
observing our fumbling attempts at life and living.

I became obsessed with *them*—
all of them, who were laid out by the winds
on that steamy June afternoon twelve years before I was born.
Their mystery stuck in me
the way romantic crushes did.
Like those attempts at love,
I would lie awake at night,
sick in my guts with longing.

Their ghosts
hovered over me—
pale and blue—
as I imagined them
in the perpetual poses of their wedding photos
and birthday party snapshots
and postured portraits—
sepia-colored—
with padded shoulders and double-breasted suits,
in full A-line skirts and crinoline—
lifted up into those winds
we came to despise
like the perfectly depicted martyrdom of saints
portrayed in icons or retablos.

It was the mystery of them
that grew within me
year after year.
It dominated my thinking
the way God
or love
or poetry
would obsess me at other times in my life.

Those ghosts hung there above me
hovering about in some distant heaven.
The oppressive air of
their presence was made more real
as I struggled one long summer to read Walter Hilton

and his eerily descriptive phrases.
I would repeat them like incantations.
"Ghostly affection," I would say.
"ghostly mirth," and
"ghostly sight," and thought I knew
what they meant.

After all,
this was my ghostly mirth.
This was my ghostly sight—
staring into the murky unknown
and seeing what others didn't.
And what I felt for them
then and always
was truly ghostly affection.

Ghosts have always obsessed me.
Even now, praying for them,
reciting for them the requiem masses most never had,
absolving what they did or failed to do,
I bond to them in that ghostly way
that I bond with anyone I bury.
And, like ghosts, we grasp at each other
across the abyss,
our voices sounding to the other
like the first rumble of approaching thunder.

North Prairie Lutheran Cemetery
near Simcoe, North Dakota

1957 seems unreal
to me in this modern moment.
And here it is
chiseled out three times
in thick granite.

On this grassy rise
I stand firm against the wind,
in my coat, with my prying camera eye,
searching the grass
and chiseled granite for votives,
for the left-behind
proof someone
existed here.
Three people lived.
They were born and grew.
Three people were carried here
in polished silence
from the violence
and found in this ground peace.

Whatever debris
the wind summoned forth
in that distant year,
that strange arrangement
of numbers,
never made it this
far outstate.

Ghosts refuse
their trek back to
grass-covered rises in
rolling distant lands.
They exist only in those
unimaginable heights,

in star-filled places with names like
Delphinus
Ophiuchus
or Canes Venatici,
names which, for all I know
are made-up, exotic as distant planets.
Their ghosts exist
in the crushing weight
of shifting air and space.

Ghosts go into their silence in agony
and find in silence a refuge.
I find silence uncomfortable this day
that moves over me like a storm front.
It is an unpleasant end
to be crushed into silence
by experience and complacency.
That is an end reserved not for young people,
not for people like this family or myself,
but for old men
and trees.

Lisa Linrud-Marcis

Communion

I

The hum of the machine is steady.
Back and forth the combine goes,
reassuring. Until my father stops it.
Sometimes it is to see how well
the wheat is threshing and sometimes
it is because the feederhouse is slugged.
Sometimes, though, he stops
his combine to scoop a handful of grain
from the hopper
just to chew it because
he likes the way it tastes.
He stands there
just outside the cab of his combine, chewing
the grain and surveying what is left:
full heads, the seeds of grain,
bran and germ for next year,
waver as a breeze sifts through stalks.

II

In the front of this small church,
in front of this small congregation
with their old smells, I kneel
in my church clothes. My knees sink
into the soft velvet cushion,
my hands stretch across the railing,
cupped and ready to receive
the wafer, watching as the pastor moves
down the line.
They are piled in a tarnished gold tray,
the points of the cross on each
stretch to the edges, quartering the wafer.

This is never the part people are excited about
at first communions. When I finally have the wafer,
it quickly dissolves on my tongue,
before taste is even possible and how difficult
it is to remove from the roof of my mouth,
where much of it clings.

III

Following the chorus of voices
repeating the Lord's Prayer
and the Benediction,
following family photos
in front of the altar,
girls in white dresses,
the congregation gathers in the basement.
Coffee and cake, another kind of
communion, sweeter
than the first. There is talk
and laughter, a sense
of something new,
a beginning without any doubts,
so sure of itself.

IV

Buy lots of flour he says to me now
because that's the business I'm in.
The business of feeding people.
From the family farm, wheat stretches
until it is nothing more than a blur of
neutral color, bland. Wheat is in the granary and
in the six steel bins behind the granary.
Wheat is loaded into the barn and
the quonsets. It is piled in the front yard.

Some of this wheat will become flour,
bread, pies, multi-grain Special K,
and Wheat Thins. And some will become
the body of Christ, the bread given
across altars.
Now, as years have passed,
when church is over and
the faithful have been fed,
I take the rest of the bread
to the basement,
greedy for more.

Anticipating the Thaw

Hard, dark soil rests
frozen, coated
with a light layer of snow.
Fields that once were
discernible by color—blue for flax,
dusty honey for wheat—
now trickle together, one to the next
to the next to the next. Every hue overtaken
and blended together until
just white.

Families again, six-o-clock dinners,
football games and social lives.
Weddings to attend—a farmer's
daughter could never be married in spring
or fall. A time free of defeat.
Men surround
the football field, arms crossed
over Carhartt jacketed chests.
They nod at each other when the home team scores,
put their faith again in what they can't control.
They gather at baptisms and funerals,
in dusty suits pulled from corners of closets;
reappear in local diners.
The pews are filled again with men.
As October slips
to March and April, they will meet
on Fridays and Saturdays,
in church on Sundays,
rehearsing bushels per acre, yields,
this harvest's disappointments—
Had to leave some of it behind—
and next year's expectations.
Gonna be a late spring this year.
Told and retold in church basements

over row after row of white tablecloths—
the narrative of every family farm,
the thaw awaiting.

Compact

I

Snow packs together tightly cloaking
dormant cropland. Crisp air stills,
emphasizes every movement crunching across
compacted terrain. Bootprints
from the workshop to the house. He follows
the same path each time, no way to tell
how many times it's been traveled.
I would guess five or six times
today. He paces from one building to another,
already planning the spring, already worrying
about the fall. From a distance
his dirty blue coat looks vibrant and new.
Smoke emerges tightly coiled from his pipe,
gets lost against the pale plain.

II

While the weather is nice
there is much to be done:
crops to be monitored,
machinery readied for harvest,
bins cleaned. Grass in the front yard
is trampled and brown, stamped in
tractor, truck and combine tread, flattened
from my father's working.
When he troubles over
engines and concaves,
he is quiet.
When he stops to eat,
he is quiet.
Grains are pushing through soil
silently, and
he is listening.

Married

They move together
all day in the sun. Man and woman
cultivating the earth, harvesting wheat.
Directions and static from the CB radio
charge the air, *We'll unload on the go* or
This one goes in the bin. Questions
about moisture and weight,
how late will the grain elevator be open or
how long until they are full. They move
as a piece of old machinery, rusted
in places.

They return home late
tired and hungry. Dirt
mixed with sweat, smeared across tanned faces
makes them difficult to tell apart.
They rewarm leftovers, casserole remnants
and tater-tot hot dishes. They pray together—a habit;
then are silent together—also a habit. Dinner is eaten
quietly. They take turns in the shower;
their filthy clothes shed, in a pile.
They ease into cotton
sheets with a soft blue floral print.
Through the open window comes cricket stridulations
and the smell of grain dust.
Man and wife
reach for one another.

Conquering

The neatly mowed yard ends abruptly
in a mound of waist-high grass and weeds.
An old farm plow
has been there since anyone
can remember. Rusted orange-red
and weather beaten,
it waits, antiquating.

It is difficult
not to imagine the horses working
with the man, muscles flexed,
breathing in dirt, drying
the inside of the mouth and nose.
Pushing and pulling *this outfit here*
through soil, breaking the crust. Conquering
acres a step at a time. He lowers and lifts,
feels how deep the seed shall rest. He tastes
the need for rain;
lungs seize for a moment, forcing
extra exertion, groans
from both horse and human.

Today, the machine's hum
cuts thick air.
The man sits, watches, monitors, adjusts.
Responds to beeps and gauges. Moves
levers delicately into position.
But he is tired and worn; his muscles
feel stiff. That's the trouble.
You had to rest the horse
so you rested the man. These machines
don't quit.

David R. Solheim

Seven Citizens

*Commissioned for Citizens' Day, 1 October 1989, in Minot,
by the North Dakota Statehood Centennial Commission.*

Farmer

Trees is all the difference
'Tween the ones just passin' through
And the one who meant to stay.
No profit in 'em. Comfort
For the eye and shelter from
Storm. Places without trees is
Where farmers just mine the land.

Miner

I spent my life in this pit,
Emptied its carbon. Now
The neighboring towns dump a
Load a day of leftovers
From lives. Mine will close before
This chasm does, but I'm laying
Down monsters I'll never see.

Grocer

Fresh from Norway, grandfather
Began the store, proud to be
A merchant. Like my father,
I left, but returned to the
Order of stacked cans, the heft
Of dry goods. I search for my
Children under cabbage leaves.

Widow

When my Henry died, I moved
Back home where Mom looked after
Me. Good days I walk downtown.
Now vines have climbed the pillars
Of the porch. In the dusty
Attic of my childhood, I
Mourn that none will follow me.

Teacher

They still return to my room.
I know them fact and fiction,
Bless their children with my smiles.
They were all my family.
In my dreams, he's still alive,
Sculpted like an ancient god,
But deep darkness hides his eyes.

Salesman

Have I got something for you.
This new one will change your life.
I can get it wholesale. Done.
Tomorrow morning when I
Get up, I'll shower and shave.
Begin the day clean and sharp.
I like living on the edge.

Transient

I seen hard times. Buildin's sway
Like boxcars in tornados.
One blizzard night in a barn
I set alone burnin' hay
And sumpthin' saved me for this
Train a-comin', but one day
I'll put down roots like you done.

Remembering My Dakota Adolescence from the Huaxi Hotel, Tonxi District, The People's Republic of China

It is forty degrees centigrade today.
I see the people working:
Hoeing fields, making bricks,
Climbing to the high terraces.
They are always moving,
Always carrying something;
A bicycle, its baskets buried in greens
A mule with a cartload of melons.

On the balcony of the apartments across the street,
Inhabitants begin using the standpipes and sinks
Built into the balustrades of the verandas.
A passing messenger hoses off his feet and calves;
A woman washes her supper greens in a basin.

While I recall the pleasure of cool water in July,
A couple scrubs their hands, and arms, and faces.
I feel the rough cloth on my skin
And the slow evaporation of the day.

Sol Departing the Prairie

On the evening
Lake, geese circle in the last
Still open water.

In shadowed stalks
Hidden black-masked pronghorns
Bedding down await.

Clattering fractals
Of shelterbelt elms reveal
Abandoned nests.

Two Views of Writing Rock

Commissioned for Native American Day, 5 April 1989, in Grand Forks by the North Dakota Statehood Centennial Commission.

I. *Northern Anasazi*

He sought his vision where the nighthawk nested.
The spirit bird's hoarse cry filled his ears,
And the whistling wings wove a circle round him.
The animals given him came to the circle.

The vision so strong, he lined in stone
The track of each visitant: bear paw and cougar,
The scratchings of turkey and grouse;
But shining in the center of the stone
The chevroned bird itself, soaring over all it gave.

He brought his sons to the nesting place,
Told his vision and showed his totem marked in stone.
They brought their sons, and they brought theirs.
Each heard and dreamed and lived his life.
The story went from "father's vision," to "grandfather's dream,"
To "an old man said," and the dream disappeared.
Only the rock remained. The bird is still so beautiful,
It weaves the circle of this story.

II. *White*

With spring snow, I came to Writing Rock.
The winter world speckled with horned larks
Seeking strength from the promise of sunshine.
Each fieldstone seemed topped by a bird
Startled into life at my approach.

The hill seemed no higher than its neighbors,
But its vision was the curve of earth.
I saw a bird preserved on stone.
The stone sheltered by rock pillars,
A re-bar cage, and wooden roof.
A living bird fluttered from the rock's ridge;
The stone bird soared though bound to earth.

Like the ones who marked the rock,
I mark my symbols on the page
Wishing to hold what escaped.

Plowing

Those Indians are gone now,
But once in a while I find
A flaked stone point, sometimes an
Earthen mound that still must hold
Clay-packed bones.

             The faint outline
Of a buffalo wallow
Disappears in the furrow,
As I erase another
Moment the land lies holding.

Heid E. Erdrich

Guidelines for the Treatment of Sacred Objects

If the objects emit music,
and are made of clay or turtle shell,
bathe them in mud at rainy season.
Allow to dry, then brush clean
using only red cloth or newspaper.
Play musical objects from time to time.
Avoid stereotypical tom-tom beat
and under no circumstances dance or sway.

If objects were worn as funerary ornament,
admire them verbally from time to time.
Brass bells should be called *shiny*
rather than *pretty*. Shell ear spools
should be remarked upon as *handsome*,
but beads of all kinds can be told,
simply, that they are *lookin' good*.

Guidelines for the treatment of sacred objects
composed of wood, hair (human or otherwise),
and/or horn, include offering smoke,
water, pollen, cornmeal or, in some instances,
honey, chewing gum, tarpaper,
and tax incentives.

If an object's use is obscure,
or of pleasing avian verisimilitude,
place rocks from its place of origin
within its display case. Blue-ish rocks
often bring about discovery, black rocks
soothe or mute, while white rocks irritate mildly.
All rocks must return to their place of origin
whenever they wish. Use only volunteer rocks,
or stones left by matri-descendant patri-tribalists.

Guidelines for the treatment of sacred objects
that appear or disappear at will
or that appear larger in rearview mirrors,
include calling in spiritual leaders such as librarians,
wellness-circuit speakers and financial aide officers.

If an object calls for its mother,
boil water and immediately swaddle it.
If an object calls for other family members,
or calls collect after midnight, refer to tribally
specific guidelines. Reverse charges.

If objects appear to be human bone,
make certain to have all visitors stroke
or touch fingertips to all tibia, fibula,
and pelvis fragments. In the case of skulls,
call low into the ear or eyeholes, with words
lulling and kind.

If the bones seem to mock you
or if they vibrate or hiss,
make certain no mirrors hang nearby.
Never, at anytime, sing *Dem Bones*.

Avoid using bones as drumsticks
or paperweights, no matter
the actions of previous Directors or Vice
Directors of your institution.

If bones complain for weeks at a time,
roll about moaning, or leave chalky outlines,
return them instantly to their place of origin,
no questions asked. C.O.D.

Little Souvenirs from the DNA Trading Post

> *A pregnancy lasts forever…because every woman who has been pregnant carries these little souvenirs of the pregnancy for the rest of her life.*
> —Dr. Diana W. Bianchi

BUT IT'S A DRY HEAT…

Touch me here and you touch her.
Cinnamon smell on the air—

                                        I've never cared much for Time…
You mean the concept of time?

GREETINGS FROM SUNNY…

Touch me here and you touch what she left in me,
what ropes me to her—

                                        Mountains made of Time, I like.
You interrupt me, darling.
You need not do so, you know.
You are with me always.

I AM FINE, WISHING YOU WERE HERE.

I hear you always, like Eiffel Tower earrings jingling in my ears,
like the silent snow in the globe,
vivid blue Seattle skyline behind—

                                        You hear me in silence?
Yes. Most certainly. Do you hear me?

My healing hands—let me put them on you...
How do you know just where it hurts?
Touch you here and I touch me.

ODDEST KNOWN REVERSAL OF MATERNITY.

Cowgirl purse, leather-worked in miniature from Out West,
stone postcard labeled Artifacts of Ancient Inhabitants...

What did you bring me?
What did you bring me?

How We Walk

Though the snow won't go and the ice takes a bit, he walks me daily. We stalk our urban pond, city buildings at one shoulder and gentle waters at the other. We walk and talk of work, laugh about the kids, then get to the business of money. Money this and money that, enough and we'll be OK, and money, money, money, until he cries "Look! Mink!" Two mink, black and burnished against the white, frozen ponds, leaping straight up and out, taking turns in hot pursuit through crusted snow. We run to the melting edge to watch them tumble, bouncing, across a thin sheet of ice so bright our eyes smart and strain. They vanish at the island's edge. We walk on, amazed, full of joy. We talk of mink tracks, ice and (a little) about money.

His eye saves me, brings me beauty daily, spots the tracks, the eggshell, the eagle as it passes, something of wonder every day. We walk this way.

How We Eat

Hot from the pan, green and garlicky—all the energy of sun turned to leaf and ours to eat. What a bear can eat, we can eat. If, lost in the wilds, we don't find a bear, we can follow raccoon's paws printing a menu in mud— nest eggs and berries, with minnows to finish. Or dig for our dinner in the dark like raccoon going for grubs in stumps. Still, we cannot be sure of everything he eats. We do not know every root, cannot trust those people. Winter roots, round and pale cheeked, drawn through earth to the moon, heave up just enough to see the moon and say, softly so we can just hear: *She is not our kind—but how kind her face. How far off and hungry her look.*

Boom

Pale wool, blue horizon design, an itchy landscape.
We all wore the same bargain sweater,
in an airplane, in a dream. Boom. A fight erupts.

Take your seats please, and can we have peace?
No more argument from you, Mr.
Mister Not-Our-Same-Sweater-Wearer.

The radio wakes me with its cultured accent:
"The Labor Department today said..."
Push. Push. Push, my beloved urges
as he snaps it to snooze.

Snow and silence fill things
with nothing. But you all know that from Stevens.

Still, stillness.

Swirls of subconscious speak still,
so early my yearning bares itself:
prairie, butte, air so huge you gulp,

you might go down, drown from so much sky.
Such perfect absence. There's nothing there but
birds whirling, snow geese as far as the eye sees.

North Dakota winds in grassland,
now that's constancy. Buffalo grass glows,
frosted, flowing, speaking low, secretive.

Used to be there was nothing there.
Close it up, they used to say.
Return it to the Buffalo. Forget Indians.

Wind churns a million watts.
Gas burns ancient marshes off.
Coal pits deep and busy, like messy little cities.

Tell you what, drive out at night.
This is what an engineer in Fargo urges.
Flares for miles, he promises, *as far as the eye…*

These are My Pearls, This is My Swine

Pale soap bubble accreted around grit.
Irritation gone iridescent, gone global.

These are my pearls, this is my swine.

Unleash the tuxedo pigs, attired so fine.
Let boars fork these pearls like truffles
tusked from prairie sand.

These are my pearls, this is my swine.
These my words, my copper mine.

Like the base who threw away
the worth of all his tribe,
wealth we sign away line by line.

These are my pearls, this is my swine.

Dress me in the blood shawl, drape the shells,
in a graduated rope around my neck.
Tell them it is time. Open the door,
invite the oil-rich and velvet-dressed swine.

These are my pearls. I have made them mine.

Poets' Biographies

Madelyne Camrud was raised on a farm near Grand Forks, North Dakota, and has lived in Grand Forks for all but two years of her married life and in North Dakota all but nine months. She received her B.A. degree in visual arts and English in 1988 and an M.A in English in 1990 from the University of North Dakota, and was awarded the Thomas McGrath Award in Poetry by UND's English Department. Camrud was employed at the North Dakota Museum Art 1991-2001 as Director of Audience Development and, later, as curator for the Museum's Art Auctions. In the spring of 2005, North Dakota Poet Laureate Larry Woiwode named her an Associate Poet Laureate of North Dakota. Camrud is working on poetry manuscripts: *A Man No Longer in the House* and *On the Way to Moon Island*. In her spare time, she makes art and works in support of the arts in her community.

Heidi Czerwiec grew up in North Carolina and studied poetry at UNC-Greensboro and at the University of Utah before moving to Grand Forks in 2005 to teach at the University of North Dakota, where she also directed the UND Writers Conference for seven years. During that time, she has traveled across the state to visit high schools as part of the Poetry Out Loud program. She is the author of two poetry collections: *Self-Portrait as Bettie Page* (Barefoot Muse, 2013) and *Hiking the Maze* (Finishing Line Press, 2010), and her poems, translations and essays have appeared in numerous journals in print and online.

Heid E. Erdrich grew up in Wahpeton, North Dakota, with seven siblings, including the authors Lise Erdrich and Louise Erdrich. She is an enrolled member of the Turtle Mountain Band of Chippewa, Belcourt, North Dakota. She attended Dartmouth College and Johns Hopkins University, and earned a Doctorate from Union Institute. Heid Erdrich is the author of four collections of poetry, including *National Monuments*, which won a Minnesota Book Award and *Cell Traffic* from University of Arizona Press. Her most recent book is a nonfiction work, *Original Local: Indigenous Foods, Stories and Recipes from the Upper Midwest*. She has won awards from the Minnesota State Arts Board, Bush Foundation, The Loft Literary Center and First People's Fund, and a City Pages Artists of the Year designation for 2013. Erdrich is also a playwright and creator of multi-disciplinary performances and films. She is a visiting artist and scholar, appearing at dozens of colleges, universities, libraries, cultural and arts organizations throughout the country each year. Erdrich teaches writing in the Low-Residency MFA Program of Augsburg College.

Dale Jacobson has published nine volumes of poetry, including *Metamorphoses of the Sleeping Beast* and the book-length poem, *A Walk by the River*, as well as critical work on Thomas McGrath. He taught a year for Vista at Sitting Bull College at Ft. Yates, North Dakota, and has taught for 30 years at the University of North Dakota. He is an Honorary Poet Laureate of North Dakota.

Rhoda Janzen was born in Harvey, North Dakota, where her father was a pastor in a Mennonite community. She has written about her heritage in the *New York Times* No. 1 bestselling memoir *Mennonite in a Little Black Dress* (Henry Holt, 2009), a finalist for the Thurber Award for Humor and for the Lily Fellows Arlin G. Meyer Prize. Janzen's sequel memoir, *Mennonite Meets Mr. Right* (Grand Central, 2012), was a finalist for Books for a Better Life Award. An English professor at Hope College in Holland, Michigan, Janzen is also the author of a collection of poems, *Babel's Stair* (Word Press, 2006).

Robert King taught at the University of North Dakota in English and Education from 1968 to 1996, when he was given the Faculty Achievement Award for Excellence in Teaching, Research, Creative Activity, and Service. The author of six chapbooks, he has published two books of poetry (*Old Man Laughing*, Ghost Road Press, 2007, and *Some of These Days*, Conundrum Press, 2014) and a creative non-fiction book about North Dakota's Sheyenne River (*Stepping Twice into the River: Following Dakota Waters*, Univ. Press of Colorado, 2005). He says, "My mother was born in Westhope, North Dakota, and spent some young years in Grand Forks, but I didn't remember that connection until she told me when I started teaching at UND in the fall of 1968. I then spent twenty-seven years on the bottom of old Lake Agassiz, taking in the big sky, the rich dark earth, the pothole prairies, the badlands, and the distances and closeness of the people of my state."

Denise Lajimodiere is an enrolled citizen of the Turtle Mountain Band of Chippewa who spent her early years raised on the reservation until her family relocated to Portland, Oregon, in the mid-'50s. She returned to the reservation to pursue her dream of teaching, graduated from the University of North Dakota with a teaching degree, and eventually went on to earn a Master's and Doctorate from UND. She works as an assistant professor in Educational Leadership at North Dakota State University. She has a deep love of North Dakota, where prairie whirlwinds are kicked up by the wings of dragonflies.

Ed Bok Lee grew up in South Korea and North Dakota, also hunting and fishing throughout Minnesota. Lee is the author of two national bestselling books of poetry and prose, *Whorled*, which won the American Book Award and Minnesota Book Award, and *Real Karaoke People*, winner of the PEN/Open Book Award. The son of Korean immigrants, he has worked as a phys ed instructor, bartender, journalist and translator, and holds an MFA from Brown University. His stories and plays have appeared widely, including at major regional and national theaters such as the Guthrie Theater, New York Theater Workshop, Joseph Papp Public

Theater, Theater Mu, Taipei Theater, Trinity Repertory Company and the Walker Arts Center.

Lisa Linrud-Marcis grew up on her family's farm north of Velva, North Dakota. Her family has been farming in North Dakota for 95 years. She received the University of North Dakota's 2011 Distinguished Thesis Award for her Master's thesis, *In Grain,* which was published as a chapbook by Finishing Line Press. She is a faculty member at Itasca Community College in Grand Rapids, Minnesota.

Debra Marquart's poetry collections include *Everything's a Verb, From Sweetness: Poems,* and *Small Buried Things.* Marquart's short-story collection, *The Hunger Bone: Rock & Roll Stories,* drew on her experiences as a traveling rock and roll musician. Her work has been widely published and received many honors, including a Pushcart Prize, the Shelby Foote Nonfiction Prize from the Faulkner Society, the Normal School Poetry Prize and a National Endowment for the Arts Prose Fellowship.

Marquart's memoir about growing up a rebellious farmer's daughter on a North Dakota wheat farm, *The Horizontal World: Growing Up Wild in the Middle of Nowhere,* was awarded the Elle Lettres Award from *Elle* Magazine and the 2007 PEN USA Creative Nonfiction Award. Marquart teaches in the Stonecoast Low-Residency MFA Program at the University of Southern Maine, and she is a professor of English and the program coordinator of the MFA Program in Creative Writing and Environment at Iowa State University.

Tim Murphy was born in Hibbing, Minnesota, and when he was six months old, he moved to Moorhead, Minnesota, where he was president of his senior class and captain of his debate team. He then went to Yale, where he was graduated as scholar of the house in poetry in 1972. He moved to Fargo in 1976. He has more than 800 poems in print, and he is completing his 14th book.

Jamie Parsley was born in Fargo, North Dakota, and was raised near Harwood, North Dakota. His first book of poems, *Paper Doves, Falling,* was published in 1992 when he was 22. Over the next 22 years, he published 11 more books of poems, including *Fargo, 1957* (2010, The Institute for Regional Studies), which chronicled the June 1957 tornado that struck Fargo, and most recently *That Word* (2014, North Star Press). He has an MFA in Creative Writing from Vermont College and in 2004, he was named an Associate Poet Laureate of North Dakota by Larry Woiwode. An Episcopal priest, he serves as Priest-in-Charge of St. Stephen's Episcopal Church in Fargo.

Aaron Poochigian was born and raised in Grand Forks, North Dakota, and lived in Fargo, North Dakota, while attending Moorhead (Minnesota) State University. He now lives in New York City, where he writes poetry in a state of non-romantic poverty. His book of translations from Sappho, *Stung With Love*, was published by Penguin Classics in 2009, and Penguin will publish his translation of the Greek epic *Jason and the Argonauts* later this year. For his work in translation, he was awarded a 2010-2011 Grant in Translation by the National Endowment for the Arts. His first book of original poetry, *The Cosmic Purr* (Able Muse Press) was published in March 2012, and several of the poems in it collectively won the New England Poetry Club's Daniel Varoujan Prize. His work has appeared in such newspapers and journals as the *Financial Times*, *Poems Out Loud* and *Poetry*.

Although **David R. Solheim** was born in Elgin, North Dakota, when his parents were teaching in nearby New Leipzig, his earliest memories are of his preschool days in Washburn, North Dakota, and visits to his grandparents' farm near Tuttle, North Dakota. Through adolescence and young adulthood, he spent most of his summers working for relatives who farmed in North Dakota.

He taught at Dickinson (North Dakota) State University for almost 30 years, during which he also traveled to and taught in the People's Republic of China. Working as a writer in residence for the North Dakota Council on the Arts and with the North Dakota Humanities Council, he has conducted hundreds of writing workshops, humanities programs and poetry readings in more than 60 communities in North Dakota and in neighboring states and Canadian provinces.

He was a recipient of the John Hove Memorial Writing Fellowship, was an international exchange artist to Winnipeg, was selected as the North Dakota Statehood Centennial Poet and continues as an Emeritus Associate Poet Laureate of North Dakota. The Territorial Press in Moorhead, Minnesota, published two chapbooks of his poetry: *On The Ward* (1975) and *Inheritance* (1987). The Northern Plains Ethnic Foundation published *West River: 100 Poems* (1989), which has since been re-issued by the Buffalo Commons Press (2007). The latter press has also published his more recent books: *The Landscape Listens: Poems* (1999) and *Green Jade and Road Men: Translations, Commentary, and Poems of China* (2011).

Mark Vinz was born in his mother's hometown, Rugby, North Dakota, where he also spent many childhood summers. He grew up in Minneapolis, Minnesota, and eastern Kansas and attended the universities of Kansas and New Mexico. He is Professor Emeritus of English at Minnesota State University Moorhead, where he served as the first (1995-98) coordinator of MSUM's Master of Fine Arts in Creative Writing program. His poems, stories and essays have appeared in numerous magazines and anthologies; his most recent books are collections of poems, *Long Distance*, *The Work Is All*, and *In Harm's Way*. He is also the co-editor of several anthologies, including *Inheriting the Land: Contemporary Voices from the Midwest*, and *The Party Train: A Collection of North American*

Prose Poetry. He is completing a collection of essays, *In Search of the Geographical Center*.

A recipient of a National Endowment for the Arts fellowship in poetry, he has also won the New Rivers Press Minnesota Voices competition, Milkweed Editions "Seeing Double" competition, six Pen Syndicated Fiction awards, three Minnesota Book Awards and the Lake Region Arts Council Individual Artist award. From 1971-1981, he was the editor of the poetry journal *Dacotah Territory*, and of Dacotah Territory Press from 1973-2007. He has done extensive work with K-12 students in the North Dakota and Minnesota Writers in the Schools programs, and given readings from his work and workshops on various aspects of creative writing and literature throughout the region, as well as several jazz and poetry performances in collaboration with pianist David Ferreira and bassist Bill Law, most recently a half-hour program for Prairie Public TV in Fargo.

Richard Watson teaches Pop Culture, Honors Classes, Communication Arts and Music History at Minot (North Dakota) State University. He has been a singer/songwriter and poet in North Dakota since 1967. He thinks of his songs and poems as "High Plains Creole." He has two books available: *The Lost Colony* and *The Lost Colony: Christmas*. Two more books, *The Spot* and *Blue Jesus*, were to be released in spring and winter 2014. He is a North Dakota Associate Poet Laureate.

Larry Woiwode's first book of poetry, *Even Tide*, was published in 1977 by Farrar, Straus & Giroux. He's been working on a new book since but prose keeps getting in the way: novels, short-story collections, memoirs, essay collections, a biography, a children's book, a commentary on *Acts* and the like. He is a Guggenheim and a Lannan Literary Fellow and has served as North Dakota's Poet Laureate since 1995.

Publication Acknowledgments

Madelyne Camrud: "Watching" first ran in *This House is Filled with Cracks* (New Rivers Press); "How It Begins," "The Day after Valentine's," "A White Ring around the Moon," and "The Bird in My House" are from *Oddly Beautiful* (New Rivers Press); "How It Begins" appeared in *Water~Stone Review* as "How Death Begins;" "The Day after Valentine's," *descant*; "A White Ring around the Moon," *Dos Passos Review*; "The Bird in My House," *New Millenium Writings*. All poems reprinted with permission.

Heidi Czerwiec: "Sedating the Cats," *New South*; "Fault. Lines," *Coal City Review*, "Cardinal Directions: Divorce Fugue," *Crab Orchard Review*; "Song Against Songs," *Measure*; "Fall Rondeau," therondeauroundup.blogspot.com. All poems reprinted with permission.

Heid E. Erdrich: "These are My Pearls, This is My Swine," *Revolver*; "Boom," *Water~Stone Review*; "Guidelines for the Treatment of Sacred Objects" first appeared in *National Monuments* (Michigan State University Press); "Little Souvenirs from the DNA Trading Post," "How We Walk" and "How We Eat" first appeared in *Cell Traffic* (University of Arizona Press). All poems reprinted with permission.

Dale Jacobson: "For Tom McGrath," "American Hitchhiking Blues," and "Grandfather Schmidt" first appeared in *Metamorphoses of the Sleeping Beast* (Red Dragonfly Press); "I Keep Returning" first appeared in *A Walk by the River* (Red Dragonfly Press); "A Moment of Clarity" first appeared in *Voices of the Communal Dark* (Red Dragonfly Press). All poems reprinted with permission.

Rhoda Janzen: "North Dakota Sestina" first appeared in *Christian Century* and appears in *Babel's Stair* (Word Press); "The Edge" *Quercus Review*. All poems reprinted with permission.

Robert King: "Late Harvesting," "Windbreaks," "Woman in the House," "The Shape of the World," and "Fourth of July" all appear in *A Circle of Land* (Dacotah Territory)

Denise Lajimodiere: "Dakota January," *Yellow Medicine Review*; "My Grandfather Was a New Initiate" appears in *Dragonfly Dance* (Michigan State University Press). All poems reprinted with permission.

Ed Bok Lee: "All Love Is Immigrant," "Mrs. Joseph B—On Love, Sin, & Celadon," and "Neon Pyramid" appear in *Whorled* (Coffee House Press); "On the Velocity of Souls" *Revolver*; "Year of the Dog" first appeared in *Mizna: Prose,*

Poetry, and Art Exploring Arab America, and appears in *Real Karaoke People* (Coffee House Press). All poems reprinted with permission.

Lisa Linrud-Marcis: "Anticipating the Thaw," "Conquering," "Married," "Compact," and "Communion" all first appeared in *In Grain* (Finishing Line Press). All poems reprinted with permission.

Debra Marquart: "Somewhere in a House Where You are Not," *Everything's a Verb* (New Rivers Press); "Beating Up the Brother" and "Dylan's Lost Years," *From Sweetness* (Pearl Editions); "Kablooey is the Sound You'll Hear" and "Silos," *Small Buried Things* (New Rivers Press). All poems reprinted with permission.

Tim Murphy: All poems used with permission.

Jamie Parsley: "North Prairie Lutheran Cemetery" and "Ghostly," *Fargo, 1957* (North Dakota Institute for Regional Studies Press); "Two," *Crow* (Enso Press); "These Men" and "The Gathering," *That Word* (North Star Press). All poems reprinted with permission.

Aaron Poochigian: "Grand Forks, ND," "Our Town," "Mrs. Pulaski's Shrine," "Stock and Bond," and "Captain Lewis at the Pacific" all appear in *The Cosmic Purr* (Able Muse Press). All poems reprinted with permission.

David R. Solheim: "Plowing" first appeared in *Southern Poetry Review*, and appears in *West River: 100 Poems* (Buffalo Commons Press); "Two Views of Writing Rock" and "Seven Citizens," *The Landscape Listens* (Buffalo Commons Press); "Remembering My Dakota Adolescence from the Huaxi Hotel, Tonxi District, The People's Republic of China," *Green Jade and Road Men: Translations, Commentary, and Poems of China* (Buffalo Commons Press). All poems reprinted with permission.

Mark Vinz: "The Doctor's Daughter" and "The Memory of Water" *Permanent Record* (Red Dragonfly Press); "North of North" and "The Last Time," *Mixed Blessings* (Spoon River Poetry Press); "Pioneer Village" *Long Distance* (Midwest Writers Publishing House). All poems reprinted with permission.

Richard Watson: All poems used with permission.

Larry Woiwode: "Crystals" first appeared under the title "Crystals from North Dakota" as the coda to the novel *Born Brothers* (Farrar, Strauss & Giroux); "Horses: V." first appeared in *Harper's Magazine* and appears in *Even Tide* (Farrar, Strauss & Giroux). All poems reprinted with permission.